Adele Getty

Goddess

Mother of Living Nature

With 141 illustrations, 16 in color

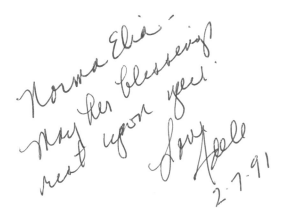

Thames and Hudson

Acknowledgments

TEXT

Robert Graves, *Adam's Rib and Other Anomalous Elements in the Hebrew Creation Myth*, Trianon Press (1955) 6; Bergerac, Photo Laborie 9; Berlin, Staatliche Museen 23; The Bridgeman Art Library 26; Photo François Varin, Explorer 11; Heraklion Museum (photo Hirmer) 13, 21; The Independent 28; Istituto Amatller de Arte Hispanico (photo Mas) 27; London, British Museum 18; London, Lambeth Palace Library 27; Milan, Castello Sforzesco 25; J. Rosellini, *Monumenti dell' Egitto e della Nubia*, Pisa (1832) 17; Paris, Musée Guimet (photo Bulloz) 31; Paris, Private Collection (photograph Jacqueline Hyde) 22; Prague, Archaeological Institute of the Czech Academy of Sciences 9; Rome, Fototeca Unione 4; Vienna, Naturhistorisches Museum 8

PLATES

Athens, National Museum of Archaeology 46; Baghdad Museum (photo Jean Mazenod, from Pierre Amiet, *Art of the Ancient Near East*, Editions Citadelles, Paris) 33; Bordeaux, Musée d'Aquitaine (photo Jean Vertut) 40; Boston, Isabella Stewart Gardner Museum 63; Damascus Museum (photo Jean Mazenod, from Pierre Amiet, *Art of the Ancient Near East*, Editions Citadelles, Paris) 50; Florence, Galleria degli Uffizi (photo Scala) 45; Werner Forman Archive 60–1; Robert Harding Picture Library 53; Colleen Kelly 48–9; C. and J. Lenars 37; Henri Lhote 49, 54; Milan, Franco Maria Ricci Collection 58; Ajit Mookerjee 42; Munich, Staatliche Antikensammlungen und Glyptothek (photo Hirmer) 55; Munich, Museum für Völkerkunde 38; New Delhi, C.L. Bharavy Collection 52; New Delhi, Pupul Jayakar Collection 34; Nara, Yakushi-ji (photo Sakamoto Photo Research Lab.) 56; New York, The Metropolitan Museum of Art, Gift of J. Pierpont Morgan, 1917 (17. 190. 185) 59; Paris, Bibliothèque de l'Assemblée Nationale 44; Paris Louvre 39; Paris Musée Cluny 46–7; Paris Musée Jacquemart-André (photo Bulloz) 51; Popperfoto 43; Private Collection (photo Alain Mahuzier, from J. Alcina Franch, *Pre-Columbian Art*, Editions Citadelles, Paris) 36; Private Collection 62; San Francisco, The Fine Arts Museum of San Francisco, Gift of Peter F. Young 64; Santa Fe, photograph Roderick Hook, courtesy of the Wheelwright Museum of the American Indian (no. P4 4A) 61; Photo Scala 41; Trier, Rheinisches Landesmuseum 35; Annie Truxell 57

THEMES

Alampur Museum, Hyderabad State 67 t.l.; Ankara Museum (photo Josephine Powell) 86 t.; Archaeological Survey of India 85 t.; Athens, British School (photo Josephine Powell) 88 t.r.; Author's Collection 82 t.; Baltimore, courtesy of the Walters Art Gallery 81 t.l.; Basel, Museum für Völkerkunde und Schweizerisches Museum für Volkskunde 91 t.l.; Boston, courtesy of the Museum of Fine Arts. Catherine Page Perkins Fund 71 t.l., James Fund and by Special Contribution 88 t.l., Gift of F.P. Warren 91 b.; Photo Bulloz 90 b.l.; Cambridge University Museum of Archaeology and Anthropology 79 m.r.; Cairo, Egyptian Museum 87 t.l.; Carlisle, Tullie House, City Museum and Art Gallery 89 b.r.; Higgins, *The Celtic Druids*, London (1829) 66 t.; Chantilly, Musée Condé (photo Giraudon) 86 b.; Chicago, Field Museum of Natural History 94 b.r.; Photo M. Chuzeville 79 t.l.; The Cleveland Museum of Art, Purchase from the J.H. Wade Fund (31.121.) 78 b.; Douglas Dickens Photo Library 75 b.; Photo Robert Edwards 69 b.r.; Fairbanks, University Museum, University of Alaska 66 b.; Photo Fievet 95 l.; Florence, Archaeological Museum 83 t.l.; Werner Forman Archive 67 b.r.; Photo Irmgard Groth 82 b.; Leo Frobenius and Hugo Obermaier, *Hadschra Maktuba* (1925) 79 b.r.; Heraklion Museum (photo Leonard van Matt) 70 b.l.; Hopi Cooperative Arts and Crafts Guild 77 m.; The Illustrated London News 80 b.; Israel Department of Antiquities and Museums (photo Hillel Burger) 68 l.; Collection, René Jacobs, West Orange, N.J. 95 b.; Colleen Kelly 95 t.; Jacqueline Klemes of Sophia Icon Studio, London 83 b.l.; London, British Museum 70 t., 72 t.l., 79 b.l., 81 b.l., 84 t.r., 90 t.l., 94 b.r.; London, Courtauld Institute 74 m.; London, Tate Gallery and private collections 72 t.r.; The MacQuitty International Photographic Collection 73 t.r.; Madrid, Museo de America (photo Jean Mazenod, from J. Alcina Franch, *Pre-Columbian Art*, Editions Citadelles, Paris) 93 m.l.; Madrid, Museo del Prado 83 t.r.; Mansell Collection 77 t.l.; Merrion Station, PA, Photograph © Copyright 1990 by The Barnes Foundation 93 t.; Mexico, D. F., Instituto Nacional Anthropologia e Historia 85 b.l., 89 t.r.; Mexican National Museum of Anthropology 70 b.r., (photo Irmgard Groth) 81 b.r., 83 b.r.; National Monuments Record 67 t.; Newcastle, Museum of Antiquities 74 t.; New York, courtesy of the Museum of the American Indian, Heye Foundation 67 b.r.; New York, The Metropolitan Museum of Art: The Cesnola Collection; purchased by subscription (1874–76) 71 b.l., The Michael C. Rockefeller Memorial Collection, Bequest of Nelson A. Rockefeller (1979) 73 b.r., Gift of J. Pierpont Morgan (1916) 87 t.r.; New York, Collection, The Museum of Modern Art 76 b.; Photo Jean-Louis Nou 76 t.; Ottawa, National Museums of Canada 72 b.l., 75 t.r.; Oxford, Ashmolean Museum 90 t.r.; Paris, Louvre 72 b.r., (photo Giraudon) 78 t., 80 t.; Paris, Musée de l'Homme 73 b.l., 84 b.l.; Paris, Private Collection 69 b.l.; P. Delougaz, *Pottery from the Diyala Region* (1952) 65; Private Collection (photo Giraudon) 75 t.l.; Rome, Museo di Villa Giulia (photo Georgina Masson) 92 b.; San Francisco, The Fine Arts Museum of San Francisco, Gift of Peter F. Young 68 r.; Santa Fe, photograph by Roderick Hook, courtesy of the Wheelwright Museum of the American Indian (no. P4 1) 87 b.; Photo Edwin Smith 77 b.r.; Stuttgart, Württembergisches Landesmuseum 79 t.r.; Syracuse Museum (photo Hirmer) 85 b.r.; Taiwan, Republic of China, Collection of the National Palace Museum 89 l.; Trieste, Civico Museo di Storia ed Arte 74 b.; Victoria, British Columbia Provincial Museum 94 m.; Vienna, Kunsthistorisches Museum 77 t.r.; Washington, D.C., National Gallery of Art. Robert Woods Bliss Collection. Loan 69 t.; Windsor, Provost and Fellows of Eton College 91 m.; Photo Roger Wood 92 t.

Contents

Holy Goddess Tellus,
Mother of Living Nature,
The food of life
Thou metest out in eternal loyalty
And, when life has left us,
We take our refuge in Thee.
Thus everything Thou dolest out
Returns into Thy womb.
Rightly Thou art called Mother of the Gods
Because by Thy loyalty
Thou hast conquered the power of the Gods.
Verily Thou art also the Mother
Of the peoples and the Gods,
Without Thee nothing can thrive nor be;
Thou art powerful, of the Gods Thou art
The Queen and also the Goddess.
Thee, Goddess, and Thy power I now invoke;
Thou canst easily grant all that I ask,
And in exchange I will give Thee, Goddess, sincere thanks.

Eulogy, 2nd century AD

Mother of Living Nature

Since time immemorial our ancestors have left sacred images of the female form. From the caves of Lascaux in France to the Balkans in Eastern Europe the art and artefacts of the Paleolithic and Neolithic, which represent humans' earliest myth-making impulses, indicate a deep reverence for life and, in particular, for the Great Mother. She is honoured as the giver and maintainer of life; out of her belly the great mystery issues forth, and to her all return. Through her Gaian body all life is sustained in homeostatic balance. Whether or not it was the Great Mother Goddess who guided our ancestors as they became conscious beings, it is a woman, as mother, who oversees each one of us from the first moments of our being. The creation myths from countless cultures bear witness to this phenomenon and to the role that the feminine principle has played in shaping the world we inhabit. The Goddess is both universal and permanent in the imagination, and she is the greatest of storytellers; throughout the world her story is woven into the lives and legends of humanity.

The Goddess has always been recognized in a variety of forms. She is the Mother of the World, Giver of Life, the great nurturer, sustainer and healer. Yet she is also the Bringer of Death, the one who grants immortality and liberation. The Goddess giveth and the Goddess taketh away. She is capable of infinite compassion in one form and of total annihilation in another. In short, she is the embodiment of what we know as life; her story is as old as life itself, for she *is* life itself. She is time – past, present and future; she is form and formlessness. She has been virgin, lover, mother and crone. She has ten thousand names and has been called 'Queen of Heaven', 'Mistress of Darkness', 'Lady of Wild Things', the 'Weaver of the Web'. Throughout the art of the world we find her as the all-powerful creative energy of the Life Force. Without her we are nothing; with her, our capacity is filled with a vital energy that carries us forward into the future.

This is the story of the Goddess as it comes down to us through time. It speaks of our most ancient ancestors and the development of the great civilizations of the world, illustrating the once supreme role of the divine feminine and her subsequent decline. The mythological perspective is but one thread in the story; the political repercussions for women and our changing attitudes towards life and Nature are also inextricably tied up with her fate.

In spite of her gradual suppression, the Goddess has never departed from our subconscious mind. Her very nature has always been a cyclical event, one embedded in the nature of life; like a comet she returns again and again.

Opposite: Tellus Mater – the Earth Mother – surrounded by symbols of her fruitful abundance. (Panel from the Altar of Augustan Peace, Rome, 13–9 BC)

5

The current return of the Goddess comes through the spirit of the environmental movement and the worldwide women's movement – and at a most timely moment; for now that the hierarchical impulse of destruction and domination has spent itself of its *élan vital* and we are faced with planetary extinction, her sustaining power is once more of the essence. No wonder, then, that today's scientific understanding of the great eco-system of the Earth is called the 'Gaia hypothesis', after the Greek Earth Mother.

The Myth of Beginnings

For I am the first and the last,
I am the honoured one and the
scorned one . . .
I am the one whom they call Life
and you have called Death.

Gnostic hymn

The question of creation is 'What can be expected to happen in a perfectly empty space?' This search for the initial life-producing impulse, which sends us travelling back through billions of years of our own deep memory, has fascinated and baffled humankind from the dawn of history. Each culture has devised its own solution to this deepest of all mysteries, and it is striking how often the feminine force is seen as the source of all life on Earth.

In Sanskrit, the manifesting power of the creative principle is known as the Goddess Śakti, meaning energy. French Indologist Alain Daniélou describes energy as the source of everything, the origin of the phenomenal world, but also the conscious plan of creation, the principle of knowledge or perception through which its existence, real or apparent, can be known. In the sacred texts of India, the Goddess is the universal creator.

> The gods approaching the resplendent Goddess Śakti asked her: 'Who are you?' She replied, 'I am the form of the immensity; from me the world arises as Nature and person. I am the Queendom, the giver of wealth, the knower of the essence of things. I come first in all rituals. The Gods have established my various abodes. My sphere is wide. I dwell in all things. From me comes the food you eat, all that you see, all that has breath, and all the words you hear. Those who do not acknowledge me destroy themselves. Study and hear what I say with respect. I am the Pleasure of Life and Humanity.'

The Pelasgian myth of ancient Greece describes the serpent as the phallic consort of the Great Mother Eurynome – a relationship distorted in the biblical myth, in which Eve's role is one not of creation, but of mere temptation. (Woodcut by James Metcalf)

Among the Kagaba people of Columbia in South America the Goddess as mother has no cult and no prayers directed to her except when the fields are sown. Then the people chant their incantations and say:

> Our Mother of the growing fields, our Mother of the streams will have pity upon us. For to whom do we belong? Whose seeds are we? To our Mother alone do we belong. The Mother of our songs, the Mother of all our seed, bore us in the beginning of things and so she is the Mother of women, men and of all nations. She is the Mother of the thunder and the Mother of the streams, the Mother of the trees and of all things. She is the Mother of the world and of the older brothers, the stone people. She is the Mother of the fruits of the Earth and of all things. She is the Mother of our dances, of all our temples and she is the only Mother we possess. She alone is the Mother of the fire and the sun and the Milky Way. She has left us a token in the form of songs and dances.

Even the creation story told in Genesis has similarities with the Pelasgian myth of ancient Greece, which, according to Robert Graves, runs:

In the beginning the world was without form and void. And our Great Mother Euronyme rose naked from the abyss and, looking about her, found that she was alone. She danced in the darkness, and by her dancing the air was set in motion. A wind blew upon her face from the north, and she took it in her hands to rub it, giving it the similitude of a speckled serpent. This same serpent lusted after our Mother and she suffered him to cast his coils about her body, and to know her. But as yet he had no name. And in process of time our Mother took the form of a dove and brooded upon the face of the water and was delivered of a great egg; which the Serpent coiled about to hatch it, so that it split open and all things were created.

Now, when our Great Mother looked upon her works and saw that they were good, she established the years and the seasons, and the months and the weeks for ever. And each week she divided into seven nights and days.

The same theme is repeated in a North American Indian creation story, which tells of a time long before any creature was born when all that existed was a calmness, as in the eye of a great storm. This calmness was called the time–space void of Great Grandmother Wakan. Wakan is an ancient memory that all creation carries within itself, now celebrated as the Beauty Way of Life. Great Grandmother embodies the creative–receptive energy of the universe. Her feminine energy, Wakan, makes love with her masculine consort, called Great Grandfather, or Skkuan. He is the liquid, conceptive serpent energy of the universe and is seen in the night sky as the Milky Way. Together they conceive a freedom child called Wakan Tanka, known as the Great Spirit or Great Mystery. From this initial trinity the physical world is manifested. The first to be born is the Sun, the second is the Earth. Again the male and the female energies of Sun and Earth make love, this time giving birth to the plants, and the plants make possible the birth of the four-leggeds, the animals. The next coupling produces the five-pointed star people, human beings. The sixth coupling creates the ancestor spirits, or all of those who have come before; this includes the mineral, plant and animal kingdoms, along with the ancestors of the humans. Together they form the seventh phase, as all of the beings of creation weave a sacred dream. Their task is to dream the dream awake.

The present scientific myth also recognizes that initially there was a great void, and what the American Indians perceive as an origin moment of cosmic love-making, physicists label the 'Big Bang'. Whatever the truth of creation, some $4\frac{1}{2}$ billion years ago our planet Earth, the beautiful blue jewel of our solar system, settled into orbit as the third planet out from our sun. Over the course of millions of years of evolution, life emerged in the form of complex systems requiring diversity and co-operation in order to ensure survival. Fifty thousand years ago the first ancestors of our own lineage began to leave traces of their beliefs and practices. As the great ice fields retreated and new lands appeared, migrating peoples started to intermingle. In France, Switzerland, Spain and Palestine tremendous caves became permanent homes for small bands of people, sanctuaries from the weather and predatory animals. Outside, the great herds and migratory birds passed; the streams and rivers were abundant with fish, and the valley floor was lush with edible plants, berries, fruit and nuts. The sun and moon moved overhead, the seasons turned, and the rhythms of womanhood revealed the cyclical nature of life, which was imprinted in the minds of all.

This awareness soon found expression in the first signs of true art. From 35,000 years BC, from the Aurignacian culture of the Paleolithic down through the agricultural Neolithic, Goddess figurines, formed from clay and ash, then fired in the hearth, or carved from bone, horn and ivory, were made in Spain, France, Eastern Europe, Russia, the Mediterranean and the Middle East. Archaeologists have unearthed numerous amulets all depicting one or other aspect of the Goddess, her breasts or vulva. These, together with steatopygous images and elongated bird-headed figures, are clearly not forms of early pornography, as many scholars once implied. The figures, found over a wide range from France to Siberia, show a consistency of shape and theme: they depict woman's bodily capacity to give birth, to bleed and heal herself every moon, to nurture and suckle, and eventually to die and be reborn. The fetishes and votive offerings of the Paleolithic were no doubt magical aids to the people and community to ensure a good birth, a bountiful supply of milk and food, or may possibly have been part of a rite of passage into womanhood.

One of the earliest objects, from Les Eyzies in south-west France, dates from 32,000 years ago. It is carved out of reindeer antler and engraved with marks that indicate a lunar pregnancy record. The same type of birth calendar has also been found among the Yurok Indians of California. Through the observation of their own cycles and of the seasonal growth of plants, it is reasonable that women would have been the first to observe the periodicities of Nature, and the recording of these internal and external rhythms could have served to form the earliest roots of science and religion.

With this growing awareness of life came an equally intense concern with death. Neanderthal and Cro-Magnon buried their dead ceremonially, often in the floor of their living space, perhaps indicating belief in an afterlife. They used red ochre to adorn both the living and the dead, and many of the Goddess figurines, including the Venus of Willendorf, were covered with it. Red ochre is representative of the life-affirming qualities of blood, the *prima materia*. People bleed only while alive, and women bleed monthly and at childbirth. The red birth-blood is the first colour each of us sees as we are born; blood is sacred, and red ochre simulates the vital energy of life and renewal. It is possible early humans thought that by covering the deceased with red ochre they could draw the life force back into them.

At Le Roc stone slabs carved with female figures were placed with the engravings lying face down on the earth to indicate that the carvings were for the Earth Mother's eyes alone, not for the pleasure of humans. The engraved stones and other objects imply that the caves were viewed as sacred, and that the Great Mother was seen as the womb and tomb of humanity. Entering a deep cave is a profound experience for most people even today. The womb-like darkness, the damp smell of the earth, evoke an ancient memory of living inside the body of another. To enter a cave is to experience a characteristic mixture of emotions – of fear, because the cave is dark and full of ancient silence; of awe, because it speaks of timeless existence; of panic, lest one venture too far between its constricting walls; and of adventurous desire to return to one's place of origin.

The abundant forms of the Venus of Willendorf reveal deep reverence for the mysterious life-giving powers of woman and the Goddess. (Paleolithic limestone figurine, h.4⅛″, Aurignacian style)

The cave, universally identified with the womb of Mother Earth, has from earliest times been used as the place for symbolic rebirth. The animals that decorate the passageways of Lascaux also reveal an intimate link between the Goddess and the hunting rites of men.

Many of the highly stylized female figurines of early cultures, such as this mammoth tusk from Dolni Vestonice (Gravettian culture), clearly have phallic connotations. The incised marks may indicate a menstruation or pregnancy record.

At Rouffignac a vast cavern, famous for its paintings of mammoths, plunges deep into the earth for over a mile; there within the cave are round, crater-like depressions in the clay. These are the 'nests' of the cave bears, who in preparing for their annual hibernation would turn round and round, making their beds for the winter. On the walls beside the clay nests are beautiful red and black imprints of the hands of children and women, outlined with ochre blown through a reed. In the very depths of the cave is a small chamber that can only be entered with the aid of a rope. All signs indicate that the cave and the long passage into its bowels were the setting for an initiation ceremony. Rouffignac, with its cave bears and red-ochred hands of women, may be the earliest link with the Artemis bear cults that emerged thousands of years later in the Mediterranean.

It is important to note that of all the human figures found in the Upper Paleolithic none is depicted with weapons, while many appear to be involved in ceremonial activity. Yet in spite of the near absence of aggression and killing depicted in the art of the Paleolithic and Neolithic, and the universal presence of life-affirming pregnant women, most of the minds of the last century have been unable to recognize the peaceful nature of the culture they have been examining. Rather, what we derive from the experts is a terrifying insight into the reality of modern, post-industrial man. In examining the various interpretations of our early beginnings and the development of the Primordial Mother, each generation of scholarly thinking has been influenced by whatever was the contemporary position held by philosophy and science. The vantage-point we start from in interpreting the art and artefacts of the roots of our past determines what we see, and it can only be the current form of the myth we are living. The writings on our ancient ancestors are full of linguistic bias against the Goddess, women, their menfolk and their way of life. The texts repeatedly refer to 'man the hunter', 'mankind', 'man the tool-maker', 'the killer ape', 'erotic-pornographic female figures' and 'fertility cults'.

For years the experts described the earliest etchings on bones, antlers and ivory as spears, harpoons and barbed arrows. Close examination of these artefacts by Alexander Marshak, however, suggests that many of these signs represent not weapons, but plants. Aggressive Cro-Magnon man has frequently been charged with the genocide of Neanderthal man, but recent archaeological evidence indicates that they lived side by side, often inhabiting the same caves, and may have interbred. Robert Ardrey praises the 'killer ape', aggression, terror and the supremacy of the weapon. Yet when we look to modern-day hunting societies we do not find savage killers mad with the lust for blood, but rather elaborate ceremonies that carry the tribe into sacred connection with the animals.

Everything we can observe from the Paleolithic indicates a peaceful, if sometimes precarious relationship with Nature and the beasts. We can only speculate on the relationship between men and women, while noting that burials honour both sexes and that even the so-called 'fertility figures' often have phallic shapes. A history of the Paleolithic suggests a culture that existed for at least 50,000 years and had as its central figure the Great Mother, who implanted in the minds of the ancestors a culture of art, a love of life, a belief in the afterlife, a symbiotic relationship with the plants and animals, and a deep respect for the natural cycles of women.

Seed and Surplus

I will sing of well-founded Gaia, Mother of All, eldest of all beings, she feeds all creatures that are in the world, all that go upon the goodly land and all that are in the paths of the sea, and all that fly: all these are fed of her store.

Homeric hymn, 7th century BC

The Neolithic agricultural revolution that first began to take place at the end of the last great Ice Age has left us with clear reminders of the role of the Goddess and the people who worshipped her. Approximately 10,000 years BC profound climatic changes occurred in Europe and around the Mediterranean. The old world and its way of life were changing as the land became more arid. In the Near East, people had abandoned the caves in favour of more permanent settlements. Human development was passing through a period of grace, a time when humankind was betwixt and between the memory of the cave, with its Mistress of the Animals, and the coming city-states. This movement away from a migratory, hunting and gathering existence towards a stable, stationary lifestyle would in the end bear witness to the Great Goddess being transformed from a primary source deity into the mother, lover and consort of the new young God who was soon to be created in the image of man.

As the early settlements developed there seemed to be no necessity to build fortified hilltop villages; in fact, many of the early villages were built in the open, and frequently in the middle of fertile valleys. It did not occur to our early ancestors to protect themselves, because there was no one to protect themselves from. If there ever was a Garden of Eden, surely it was at this moment, when game and grain in abundance were free for the taking. This pattern of open development is recorded in the Middle East, in India, China and in Eastern Europe, and some of these cultures show signs of peaceful existence lasting well over a thousand years: unarmed, unfortified settlements that knew nothing of war, rape, plunder or invasion. And in all of these early developments the Goddess was primary.

The city of Jericho, radiocarbon-dated to 9550 BC, was founded at the site of a sacred spring – Nature's way of expressing her milk so that all might be nourished. Inside every house were images of the Goddess, and in a nearby settlement a stone carved with breasts was found in the remains of a temple. The construction of the entire site indicates a profound relationship with the Goddess: the settlement, which was initially unfortified, was built in the shape of a crescent moon, and the houses were in the form of beehives –

Women of West Africa celebrate a menstruation rite, brandishing sickles that remind us of a continuing association between woman's fertile moon-cycle and Nature's cycle of harvest plenty.

both potent and enduring symbols of the Great Mother. Throughout the world people have associated the moon with the eternal feminine, for the moon's monthly cycle is a reminder of the rhythms of womanhood. The moon represents the ebb and flow of birth, growth and death, a pattern of perpetual renewal that is made visible in the three phases of the Goddess as Maiden, Mother and Crone. In India the crescent moon was thought to be the receptacle for menstrual blood from which women produced children as the fruit of their womb; the Persians recognized the moon as the mother 'whose love penetrates everywhere', while among the Sioux Indians the moon was called the 'Old Woman who Never Dies'. The numerous crescent stone sickles found at Jericho may indicate a further connection of the Goddess with the plants that they were used to harvest.

The bees, who pollinated these plants and created nourishing nectar, were also seen as emissaries of the Great Mother. Jericho was an oasis of the Goddess's good will, in that she provided both milk and honey in the midst of the desert, and as bees require a queen to maintain the life of the hive and the production of honey, so the people of Jericho looked to their queen for protection and plenty. Later, Demeter would be known as the pure Mother Bee, her priestesses as *melissae* (Latin, 'bees'); beehive tombs have been found in Greece and Ireland, and there too they are recognized as the property of the Goddess. The ancients who constructed Jericho utilized the symbolic nature of the Goddess in such a way as to draw her into a sacred form of architecture.

In Turkey, the site of Çatal Hüyük reveals startling evidence of Goddess-worshipping peoples. Excavated for the first time in the early 1960s by James Mellaart, Çatal Hüyük flowered between 6500 and 5700 BC, predating the more famous cities of Mesopotamia by three or four millennia. The site shows no evidence of warfare or weaponry for over 800 years and was eventually deserted without any signs of deliberate violence. Of the 139 rooms excavated at Çatal Hüyük, 48 are shrines to the Goddess. They indicate an established pattern of worship that reveals the central importance of birth and death. There are large reliefs of the Goddess giving birth to bulls, while one mural shows vultures attacking the bodies of the dead. On the walls are the skulls of boar, vulture, fox and weasel enclosed in plaster reliefs of a woman's breast; the teeth, tusks or beaks of the animals protrude where the nipple should be. These toothed breasts may represent both the nurturing and devouring nature of the Mother Goddess, in that all

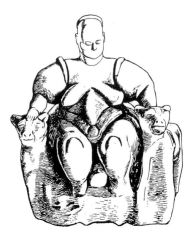

A clay statuette of the Goddess enthroned with her leopards, found in a shrine at Çatal Hüyük – perhaps the earliest representation of Cybele as the Mistress of Animals. (Line drawing by Grace Huxtable)

of her children eventually return to her. The particular animals used in making these strange reliefs are quite likely the totem animals of the various clans, in which case at the moment of death each soul was probably seen as being guided by its totemic power to the world beyond. Before burial, the corpses were left to be stripped clean by scavenging vultures, and in this we may see evidence of their association with purification and rebirth; for to the ancient mind the vulture was an ambivalent symbol, representing the twin aspects of the Great Mother: her capacity for death and destruction, and – as in the case of Egyptian Isis – for maternal solicitude.

The close association of the Goddess with wild beasts is also evident in a terracotta figure from Çatal Hüyük of c. 5750 BC showing the Goddess as Mistress of the Animals – perhaps the earliest representation of the Goddess Cybele. She is seated upon a throne; her breasts, belly and hips are enormous, and between her generous legs she appears to be giving birth. On either side of her is a leopard, and her hands rest affectionately and confidently on their heads. This is the Lady of Wild Things, who is at one with Nature and can befriend the untamed and dangerous. This theme appears repeatedly for thousands of years and in every culture: the Goddess with her wild lions, wolves, deer, snakes, birds and bears, who seem to offer themselves into her service. Perhaps initially she was a clan mother who actually suckled the young leopards, as the Ainu of Japan are known to suckle and raise bear cubs. The Australian Tiwi people also bring young orphaned animals into camp and suckle them; if the animal survives the night they become part of the clan, are given a name, and are even provided with funeral rites when they die. One thing is certain, that the Goddess as Mistress of the Animals was to provide a rich legacy: she will become Cybele flanked by her lions; in Greece she will be Artemis accompanied by her hounds; she will stand in front of the temples as a prophetess with snakes coiled around her arms; and Hecate will guard the crossroads with her black dog. In the New World White Buffalo Woman will bring the message of salvation to the Plains Indians; in the Southwest Spider Woman will create the world and maintain its life through her constant spinning and weaving; and in Hawaii Pele, the Goddess of the volcano, is still seen before an eruption walking the lava fields with her white dog.

Also for the first time at Çatal Hüyük we discover the Goddess in her triple aspect as Maiden, Mother and Crone. Up until this moment the Goddess had always been portrayed as a whole, fertile mother-woman, who contained all and returned all to the source of life. Humans' growing understanding of the linear nature of time – past, present and future – had found its way into the feminine. The communal, collective mind of the past was beginning to shift, creating a more individualized view that perceived the world in time. The impulse to parcel the Great Goddess out into more and more distinct aspects of herself would continue for millennia, each facet of her great self set up as a Goddess in her own right, until the present moment, when contemporary women find the Goddess presented to them as a form of psychological puzzle, in which dozens of 'archetypes' have to be pieced back together, in order to recreate the full scope of the feminine.

Perhaps the strangest aspect of Çatal Hüyük art is that there are no phallic images or vulvas depicted. Mellaart's interesting, though not entirely convincing hypothesis is that this is because Neolithic woman was the originator of the religion, and that sex in art is generally associated with male impulse and desire. Instead, the breast, navel and pregnant belly represent the female, while the bull, stag, ram and horns symbolize the male. The importance of the Goddess in Çatal Hüyük cannot be underestimated, but her presence shows no sign of dominance over the male, for she is always accompanied by bulls, rams or stags. One piece of sculpture shows a couple hugging, and attached to it is a sculpture of a mother and child, indicating, perhaps, that the male role in conception was already recognized and acknowledged, even by this early date.

Two hundred miles away from Çatal Hüyük is the site of Hacilar, which dates from about 5600 BC. In addition to the hundreds of beautifully designed and painted pieces of pottery excavated there, exquisitely stylized sculptures of the Goddess were found. Indeed, all of the representations of human figures discovered in Hacilar are of women or Goddesses. Here we can clearly see her as Maiden, with a long braid down her back, as Mother, with a child at her breast, and as Crone, with pendulous breasts and her hair tied up in a bun at the back. Again the Goddess is portrayed with her leopard totem, and she is also found seated in the company of another Goddess or child. As at Çatal Hüyük, bulls outnumber every other animal, and there appears to be a balance between the male and female energies. As Mellaart says, 'one thing that is clearly indicated in the religion of Hacilar is the predominance of the women'. Hacilar was destroyed, probably by fire, around 5250 BC, and by 5000 BC was deserted, never to be inhabited again.

Marija Gimbutas, in her pioneer work *The Goddesses and Gods of Old Europe*, was able to substantiate an independent Neolithic culture in south-eastern Europe, dating from 7000 to 3500 BC. From Czechoslovakia and the western Ukraine to the Black Sea, and down to the Aegean and Adriatic, a highly developed civilization emerged. The Balkan area gave rise to the people of Thrace, who influenced later developments in Mesopotamia and, in the Aegean, Minoan Crete. These people were not part of a cultural backwash from the Near East, as previously thought, but part of a tradition that extended into the Paleolithic and which seems to pre-date developments in the Near East. Here once again the importance of the female principle of life and generation is echoed loud and clear, but unlike Çatal Hüyük, where the symbol of the snake is conspicuous by its absence, in south-eastern Europe the snake and the bird are the primary motifs of the Great Goddess.

The Goddess has always been on the most friendly of terms with serpents, and throughout the world she is associated with them and with the bird that wings its way into higher realms. The relationship of the snake and bird is part of the ancient shamanic rites of ecstasy, in which the initiate experiences the awakening of the coiled serpent that lies at the base of the spine. It then ascends the bodily Tree of Life, up through the trunk of the central nervous system, transforming itself into a bird which eventually takes flight and carries the shaman into the world of the divine ones. The transformational connection between the snake with its scales, and the bird with its feathers is best embodied in the Mayan story of the plumed serpent Quetzalcoatl. In addition, the snake is capable of shedding its entire skin and thus finding itself reborn — a reflection of the Goddess's capacity for regeneration. In Egypt the bird aspect of the Goddess's energy became

The Goddess of Minoan Crete, a beneficent protector of the home, holds aloft her faithful snakes – symbols of immortality and regeneration – while a bird keeps watch upon her head. (Knossos, c. 1600–1580 BC)

A bronze finial from Luristan clearly demonstrates the connection between fertility and the moon, represented by the curved horns of the ibex.

Nekhbet, the vulture Goddess, who was worshipped as a protector of childbirth. Her snake counterpart was Ua Zit the cobra, who brought increase to the green things of the land. Together they became part of the royal insignia and were known as the 'Two Ladies' who united and protected Upper and Lower Egypt.

In India two pre-Aryan cultures reveal a storehouse of evidence regarding the worship of the Goddess. In the Indus valley two comparatively large cities developed: Mohenjo-daro along the Indus river and, 400 miles away in the Punjab, the city of Harappa. Although they occur later chronologically, during the third millennium BC, developmentally they parallel what was taking place in Europe and the Near East. It is obvious that the primary deity is once again the Great Mother Goddess. The dominant agricultural need was one of fertility, and the numerous figures discovered in both cities are almost exclusively female. They have been classified by Sir John Marshall into three primary types: Mother Goddesses with a child in their arms, or pregnant women; bird-headed Goddesses with their hands on their breasts; and semi-nude figures with an elaborate crescent-moon-shaped headdress, a girdle around their loins, and jewelry in the form of necklaces and earrings. In addition to these types, Goddess figures have been found representing the Terrible Mother with a skull-like face, the one who devours life. A few figures depict the yoni, or vulva, and some show the Goddess with what appear to be goats' horns on her head – a universal symbol of renewal often associated with the crescent moon. On seals or stamps not unlike those later found in Mesopotamia and Crete, the Great Mother is also seen with the Tree of Life or holding various animals.

As these cultures developed, so did ever more elaborate fortifications around the cities. After a thousand years of continuous development in art, architecture, pottery and municipal planning, the sophisticated cultures of the Dravidian peoples of Harappa and Mohenjo-daro met an end with the arrival of the patriarchal Aryan invaders c. 1700 BC. Ironically, the caste system that was set up by the Aryans, or Brahmans, forbidding the intermarriage of the 'sons of light' with the dark-skinned Dravidians, allowed the Goddess to survive in India up to the present day – for the natives of India have never ceased to worship the Great Goddess in all her manifestations.

Each of these early cultures startled the archaeological world. It was not simply the number of Goddess figures found or the special role that the female played in each culture, but rather the level of sophistication in art and lifestyle. More startling still was the length of time these cultures existed in peace – a thousand years or more of unbroken peaceful existence is regrettably almost unimaginable to the modern mind – for these early agricultural settlements carried with them something of the old Paleolithic: a deep reverence for life and for the feminine deity who manifested abundance, fertility and increase in all she touched. The apparently egalitarian and non-hierarchical structure of these cultures is suggestive of what J.J. Bachofen believed were the essential characteristics of a matriarchal society.

What was it that caused the decline from this harmonious model of co-existence to the aggressive, competitive urges that inspired the increasingly violent struggles of the 2nd millennium BC and countless conflicts down to the present day? Ironically, the answer may lie in the very development of agriculture that seemed to offer the human race so much. The effect of early agriculture on the human community certainly deserves the title of 'Neolithic Revolution', and it is generally accepted that women were the source of this revolution, through their first-hand knowledge of plants and the rhythms of Nature. But it may be that in this development women laid the ground for their eventual domination and suppression, for although agriculture is generally deemed a fundamental breakthrough, it is important not to overlook the tens of thousands of years when people lived as nomads, foraging with a sophisticated knowledge of plants, animals and seasonal changes. With the beginnings of cultivation, the ecological balance of an area began to suffer, and, as populations grew, depletion and exploitation of the environment became a way of life. For the first time people became susceptible to drought, famine, flood and blight in a way never known before. Surpluses became a form of protection from potential disasters, while time and the future began to take on a new meaning and new importance. Humankind had been expelled from the Garden of Innocence.

The domestication of animals was also of prime importance in the Neolithic revolution, and it is to this moment that we can clearly trace the origin of paternity rights. Animal-breeding brought with it a clear realization of the male's role in the life-making process, and domination of the animals gradually resulted in the urge to 'domesticate' and subjugate women and the Goddess. One of the primary requirements for animal management is the killing or castration of unwanted males. The origins of the Sacred Bull doubtless go back to this practice of selecting one powerful bull to inseminate the entire female group while the other males were excluded; for the human males this must have been an anxious moment and the actual source of what Freud would call the 'castration complex'. It would have been impossible for the men not to apply the concept of selective breeding to themselves, and this awareness must have further destroyed the male hunting bond, as certain men asserted themselves, and others were forced to comply with the more aggressive and stronger rule of their brothers. The mutilation inflicted upon the animals was soon turned into circumcision rites for male children. It was but a short step from the Sacred Bull to the divine right of kings. Previously, animals had been seen as brother or sister creatures; the tendency of humans to organize themselves into clans with totem animals attests to this kinship. With domestication, however, animals in a sense became the first slaves. Human values were changing under the combined influence of animal husbandry, plough agriculture and population increase. The exchange of disposable surpluses and marketable goods in the newly developing city-states led to social stratification and more centralized political control, and wealth became desirable for its own sake. The possession of slaves represented the ultimate measure of both wealth and power.

The ancient and honoured role of woman was in the process of being fundamentally altered. The generation of life and its inherent joy, as expressed through the Goddess Śakti and the birth of Pleasure, daughter of Psyche and Cupid, were about to be ignored. The Goddess, as the Pleasure of Life, reveals the joy embedded in the entire body, mind and spirit. This is a sensual feeling of well-being and connectedness that places us in a state of joyful agreement or mutual understanding. In the past fertility had been associated with generation; woman formed the connection between the ancestors and future generations, for it was through her that life passed. With the awareness of paternity that came with the domestication of animals, woman began to be viewed as a receptacle for the male seed. Fertility was now inverted from generation to production. Like the cows in the field, women would have their sacred bull-king, as the men usurped the generative function. This marks the first sublimation of the feminine by the masculine, as inheritance rights began to be passed from father to son, rather than through the mother's line. Bachofen aptly calls this patriarchal inversion the 'counter-factual metaphor of male pro-creativity'.

Until this moment sex was something to be enjoyed, without social stigma attached. There were no illegitimate children or scarlet women, because there was no value in paternity. 'A child of one is a child of all', so sing the Ibo of Africa. Along with the pleasure of sex there must have been a mystical element as well, for numerous accounts of sacred sex or Tantra come down to us from classical times. From the Dionysian rites of Greece to the Tantric temples of India, a story is told that sings the praises of the transcendent nature of the orgasm. The birth of 'civilization' was the birth of patriliny and of the subjugation and perversion of women's and men's sexuality. When a Jesuit missionary reprimanded a Montagnais Indian for not stopping his wife from sleeping with another Indian, by saying 'How will you know that her children are your own?', the Indian's poignant reply was 'Thou hast no sense. You French love only your own children, but we love all the children of our tribe.'

The Divine Embrace

'Oh my Queen, Queen of the Universe, the Queen who encompasses the universe, may he the King enjoy long days at your holy lap.'

Sumerian text

With the development of writing in the Fertile Crescent – the area around the Tigris and Euphrates rivers – we begin to learn the names and titles of the Goddess. It will no longer be necessary to call the female statues 'fertility figures' or to speculate on their use for 'unknown ritual purposes'. In Babylonia she is called Ishtar; among the Phoenicians she is known as Astarte or Ashtoreth, in Cilicia, as Ate; and in India she is called Aditi.

The Goddess appears in culture after culture with a multitude of names; her pantheon is vast and her domain wide. Our early ancestors were polytheists and pantheists; there was no one all-powerful deity ruling over the lives of humanity but rather a multi-faceted Goddess who could be called upon by name to satisfy the needs of the people. Her shrines were found everywhere, for everywhere is her abode – near the hearth, at the sacred well or spring that provides water for drink and healing, in the ancient grove of trees forming Nature's cathedral, in the deepest cave, on the highest mountain. The plants and animals, the moon, sun and stars, the river that flows to the sea and the ocean itself: all were her domain. All were sacred to the Goddess. All were recognized as forming part of the Great Mother and therefore as kin.

In Egypt, the Goddess was always a vital aspect of the Egyptian pantheon. In dynastic times the vulture Goddess Nekhbet was to be differentiated into Nut, the sky, and Neith (one of the ancestors of the Greek Athene), she who existed from eternity, who created the world and placed the Sun God Ra in the heavens. In the best known of her many forms she was winged Isis,

Trees have long been sacred to the Goddess: the fig was sacred to Ishtar, the palm was the dwelling-place of Astarte, while the willow was the emblem of the virgin aspect of Hecate. Here the Egyptian Earth Mother as the Tree of Life distributes the food and drink of immortality to her worshippers. (Wall painting, 13th c. BC)

celebrated as the 'Oldest of the Old', who established the healing arts, agriculture, law and justice, and the kingship itself. For her name means 'throne', and it was through her that the pharaohs gained their right to rule, for in Egypt all property rights passed through the mother's line to her daughters. Ancient writers such as Herodotus and Diodorus reveal that the supremacy of the Goddess went hand in hand with the importance of women in Egyptian life and the great respect paid to them.

In Anatolia the Great Goddess Cybele, Cybebe or Kubaba has a history reaching back into the Neolithic. There, as elsewhere, she was the Mountain Goddess, 'Creatrix of All Things'. In classical times her myth tells of her falling from the skies as a meteoric stone, her most sacred epiphany, or describes her as a bisexual being of so dangerous a nature that it had first to be made helpless with wine and castrated. We find the name again in the Elamite Goddess Humban, and in the Babylonian demon, Humbaba, also called 'Fortress of the Intestines'. Like her nature, her name seems to be composed of two elements: Cu, as in the Indian Goddess of generation Kunti, and Baba, which means baby, dildo and phallus.

In Sumer the Goddess's name was Inanna and she sat upon the throne at Nippur, the cultural and spiritual centre of the kingdom. In her we see the ancient Mother Goddess, who received all mortal beings into her cave of death and rebirth, transformed into a heavenly power that descends 'from the great above to the great below' in order to rescue the power of life from the underworld. In the earliest Sumerian tales her creative power is allotted to Ninhursag, 'She who gives Life to the Dead', otherwise celebrated as the Lady of the Mountain, and variously called Mah, Ninmah, Nintu and Aruru. It is her image that we must see in the earliest graves near Ur, clay figures of a woman sometimes carrying a child. She is occasionally accompanied by a male figure dressed in a long robe. He is no doubt the prototype of Dumuzi, the spirit of vegetation, thought of as her son, her brother or her spouse, whose death was mourned first by Ninhursag, then by Inanna, Ishtar, Cybele and lastly by the Virgin Mary.

Early seals show the Goddess imprisoned alone in an underworld cavern, a fate later meted out to the storm God Marduk in Babylonia; and in tablets 4000 years old we can read of the descent of Inanna, Goddess of Sacred Love and of the Morning and Evening Star. It is a hymn with much significance which prefigures many of the myths of later cultures. It tells of the sacred marriage rite, where Inanna calls her lover Dumuzi to her bed:

> He shaped my loins with his fair hands,
> The shepherd Dumuzi filled my lap with cream and milk,
> He stroked my pubic hair,
> He watered my womb.
> He laid his hands on my holy vulva,
> He smoothed my black boat with cream,
> He quickened my narrow boat with milk,
> He caressed me on my bed.
>
> Now I will caress my high priest on the bed,
> I will caress the faithful shepherd Dumuzi.
> I will caress his loins, the shepherdship of the land,
> I will decree a sweet fate for him.

After the sacred marriage Inanna abandons her temples throughout the land in order to be initiated into the underworld rites of eternal transformation and rejuvenation. She must journey into darkness and pass through seven gates of initiation before returning to the world above. In the underworld Inanna's dark mirror and sister, Ereshkigal, looks upon her with the Eye of Death.

> Inanna was turned into a corpse,
> A piece of rotting meat,
> And was hung from a hook on the wall
> For three days and nights.

Whereupon, with the help of her attendant Ninshubur, the Goddess arises from the dead, becoming the first known traveller to return from the underworld. The epic poem of Inanna is the oldest extant myth that speaks of the ability to die and rise again, telling all that to die the mystic death while still alive is to achieve liberation in their lifetime. This theme of initiation, death and resurrection would be told again in Babylon with the Goddess Ishtar, in Greece with Persephone and Demeter, later with Dionysus, and eventually in the New Testament.

In ancient Sumer women originally held power in the emerging priestly hierarchy, and records show that there were many more women priests than men. Since Sumer was a theocracy, the women religious leaders were also the political officials. The arts, education, script, science and accounting were under the jurisdiction of the Goddess Nidaba, and medicine was under the guidance of the Goddess Gula. But the increasingly hierarchical structure of society and gradual centralization of power, provoked by the needs of a growing population, began to erode the egalitarian and matrifocal kinship groups of the old order, opening the door for the overthrow of the Queen of Heaven. The role both of the Goddess and of ordinary women was diminished as powerful men took control of the city-states and united them into ever larger kingdoms. The existing infrastructure of the elite soon began to use its priestesses and queens as pawns in establishing the divine right of kings.

This power shift is clearly reflected in the myths of the time, in which the relationship of the Goddess with her son/lover, first recorded in the epic poem of Inanna, is used to transform the supreme Mother of the World into the wife/mother of the emerging God/king. The process is evident in the case of the Goddess Humban of Elam, for example. In the 3rd millennium BC her male consort In Shushinak is known as 'Father of the Weak'; by the middle of the 2nd millennium political and religious changes have obviously come over Elam, for he now holds the title 'King of the Gods'; and by the 8th century BC he is 'Protector of the Gods of Heaven and Earth'. The change in emphasis away from the Mother of all Beings and towards the exalted male hero is especially clear in the story of Tiamat. Tiamat was the formlessness out of which creation came into being, the darkness before the light, and has been called Chaos. She was the mother of the female elements – Water, Darkness, Night and Eternity – and in Genesis she is called Tehom, the Deep. Among the Arabs, the Red Sea is called Tiamat; and according to Barbara Walker, the Red Sea is the reservoir of Tiamat's menstrual blood, which flowed for three years and three months. For the Sumerians she and her

This carved Sumerian bowl (c. 2700 BC) may show the Goddess Tiamat flanked by her snakes and leopards. Patriarchal pressures were to transform her from a benevolent deity into the Dragon of Chaos, slain by her own son Marduk.

family were peaceful and benevolent deities who created mankind without requiring strife or sacrifice. With the Akkadians all is changed: she becomes a huge, loathesome dragon figure. And, critical to the story of the Goddess, she is the first to be murdered by her own son Marduk. Marduk is thought to have been jealous of his brother Kingu, who was chosen to be consort in his place, and in a fit of rage he slays Tiamat and divides the firmament. In the *Enuma Elish* of the 2nd millennium BC it is recorded that after Marduk had most viciously slain Tiamat 'he split her like a shellfish, in two halves; set one above, as a heavenly roof, fixed with a crossbar; and assigned guards to watch that her waters above should not escape.' Out of the body of the slain Mother Goddess, the warrior God creates the world from an act not of generation but of matricide.

Once the creative spirit had been conceived as masculine, the numerous goddesses and gods of the past were eventually assimilated into the one God who reigns supreme. The Goddess's son/consort therefore laid the ground not only for the demise of the sacred feminine, but also for the emergence of monotheism. Soon a lone God would mechanically create the world, shape man from the dirt and woman from his rib. This usurping of the Goddess's natural gift of birth and its perversion into an act of wilful creation, whereby the masculine energy is responsible as a solitary and omnipotent force, is the second sublimation of the feminine by the masculine. The Great Mother Goddess who gave birth to the cosmic egg of the universe would now be persecuted and denounced, her temples destroyed and her followers slain.

Sons of Light

I have come to destroy the works of the female.

Gospel according to the Egyptians

It was not only changes within the structure of society itself that brought about the de-throning of the Goddess. For thousands of years groups of northern invaders had been continuously working their way south. These aggressive and war-like peoples, generally referred to as Aryans or Indo-Europeans, Kunda or Kurgans, are thought to have originated in Russia and the Caucasus region, or perhaps much earlier in the Upper Paleolithic in the area of northern Europe, and specifically Denmark. What is known is that successive waves of migration took place, probably beginning in the Goddess-worshipping centre of the Vinča culture of Europe as early as the 5th millennium BC. There, according to Marija Gimbutas, they destroyed the earliest flowering of the culture of Old Europe.

The Aryans are frequently represented as bearded warriors riding in horse-drawn chariots and wielding iron battle axes, but their most devastating weapon was the father God they carried with them and the crusade-like holy war they waged against the Goddess. Unlike the ancient Great Mother of the black-as-night caves of the Paleolithic and the womb-like temple shrines of Çatal Hüyük, their God was a God of light, flaming on the mountain-top or in the shining sky. Several authors suggest that the image of such a sky deity may have arisen from volcanic eruptions and the powerful destruction they bring as they hail down fire, rocks and lava. There may also have been meteoric showers from the heavens which captured the imagination away from the Earth and focused awe and worship upon the celestial firmament. Wherever the Aryans spread, the primary enemies of their God were the Mother Goddess and her polytheist, animistic peoples.

The politics involved in deposing the Goddess from her millennia-old position were simple. She was already accompanied by her son/lover/consort, who had assumed the role of Master of the Animals and in many places already occupied the throne as king. In order to eliminate the Goddess from the pantheon altogether, one tactic was to transform her into a demon, a serpent-monster or a dragon to be slain, and wherever a serpent or dragon is mythologically reported it is generally safe to assume it is an allegory for the old religion of the Goddess. In India the Indo-Aryan *Rig Veda* tells of the slaying of the 'serpent demon' Goddess Danu by the Lord of the Mountain, Indra. In Babylon, as we have seen, the 'son of the sun' Marduk murders his dragon mother Tiamat; the Hebrew God Yahweh destroys the serpent monster Leviathan. The sons of Gaia, Typhon and Python, are killed by the mountain/storm God Zeus and by Apollo, the sun God. Accounts of Saint Patrick driving the snakes out of Ireland to establish Christianity, and of Saint George slaying the dragon are all part of the same story.

As the male deity was viewed as the bearer of light, a further ploy in the battle against the Goddess was to equate the darkness of the cave – and therefore the womb – with evil, and soon numerous battles were being waged across the civilized world between the forces of light and darkness. On a more practical level, the patriarchal invaders sought to impose their authority by eliminating women from the temples, as priestesses, and from prominent positions in society, and by seeking to establish a system of father-right. When these tactics failed, as they so often did, genocide became the answer.

The transformation of the Goddess from the bountiful source of life into the enemy of the new God carried with it a perfidious implication: if the Goddess and her domain of moist darkness were evil, then all womankind was also evil and guilty of transgression by birth. The logical conclusion of such thinking is most clearly revealed in the world of Yahweh's patriarchs. The role of the mother is devalued, and in its place the male's reproductive power, viewed as fertile 'seed', is blessed by God as if it were self-generating. The purity of the male seed must be guaranteed through the virginity of the bride, so marriage as an institution becomes the will of God; absolute submission to God's will, and the consequent acceptance of woman's position as subservient to that of her husband are obligations that come with the Lord's covenant.

No longer do the invaders attempt to blend their pantheon with that of their 'hosts'. In Deuteronomy, Yahweh issues a command to his people: 'You must completely destroy all the places where the nations you dispossess have served their gods, on high mountains, on hills, under any spreading tree; you must tear down their altars, smash their pillars, cut down their sacred poles, set fire to the carved images of their gods and wipe their name from that place.' The Goddess is perceived as an abomination, and all of the natural functions of life – the proper realm of the Goddess – are seen as 'unclean'. In Leviticus a woman must be ritually cleansed after childbirth in order not to defile those around her. How different from Çatal Hüyük where the Goddess was seen giving birth on the temple wall, with the bull, symbol for the man, on the opposite wall! Women have been reduced to the level of breeders, and their masters want their stock seeded with no seed but their own. Sexual pleasure is now tainted by the wrath of the Lord.

The new order of Yahweh's patriarchs that was establishing itself in the name of 'morality' left much to be desired, yet the moral code of the Western world now rests upon the Bible, with its God who wilfully created the universe and gave to the 'sons of men' divine sanction to rule over the Earth and over all her creatures. Women, animals, natural resources, even the Earth Mother herself would become part of a system of acquisition and assets. Women and the Goddess were excluded from the decision-making process, for only males were allowed into the inner sanctum of the temple for generations to come.

The Patriarchal Inversion

The mother is not the parent of the child which is called hers. She is the nurse who tends the growth of young seed planted by its true parent, the male.

Apollo in the *Oresteia*

A Cretan Goddess, enthroned in a temple, her arms upraised in an ecstatic gesture. (Clay model from central Crete, c. 1100–1000 BC)

It is in the archaeological evidence and mythological texts of the Greek world that the disempowerment of the Goddess is most clearly recorded. Ironically, it is through this legacy to the Western world that we are able to gain a glimpse of who the Goddess was, and what she represented to the antique mind.

In the 3rd and 2nd millennia BC the Goddess found exuberant expression in the art of Minoan Crete. The brightly coloured pottery and frescoes depict in free and elegant line both complex ceremonial practices and the beauties of Nature, expressing an inherent joy in the mystery of existence which surely reflects the harmonious relationship to life that the people experienced in their everyday activities. The murals and artefacts of Crete indicate that the island was overwhelmingly a Goddess-worshipping centre; for a thousand years or more, until Crete was settled by the patrilineal Myceneans, the Minoans were matrilineal, and Greek scholars such as Sinclair Hood comment on the role of women as rulers and priestesses. As a sea-going people, the Minoans had from early times established their power throughout the Aegean, whose people, like themselves, were matrilineal and Goddess-worshipping.

Throughout this area the new year was celebrated according to the ancient calendar, whose fixed point was the heliacal rising of the dog star, Sirius. In Egypt this heralded the rise of the Nile, and as in Crete it was a time for the making of alcoholic drinks – of wine, beer and, more anciently, mead or fermented honey. In Crete this festival was celebrated in the Dictaean cave with a nocturnal bonfire to be seen from miles around; here their Goddess Rhea was said to give birth to her son, variously called Zagraeus the Hunter – whose myth is known to us in that of Orion – or Zan. He is the ancient form of Dionysus, the wine God. Conceived by the Goddess in an encounter on the mountain-top with the elemental spirit of light and storm, he was to be torn apart by the Titans almost as soon as he was born, as befits a God who brings about intoxication and orgiastic behaviour.

Crete was the major outpost of Anatolian civilization, and in this and other stories we recognize the major features of Goddess worship in the Middle East and beyond. The story of the dying God is a variation on that of the Lady of the Mountain, Dictynna, another form of Cybele, who like her is presented as Mistress of the Animals, flanked by her lions; her sacrificial animal is, as ever, the bull. Her son/consort Zagraeus, named after an Anatolian mountain, suffers the same fate as Attis, Adonis and even Osiris. This dying God, in whom Frazer saw the precursor of the founder of Christianity, is known as the first-born and as the one of double birth, in that the annual celebration of his birth perpetuates the moment when the Goddess first brought the world into being. His worship, which is accompanied by dances, Maenadic frenzy, and a sacrifice not to be spoken of, includes the re-enactment of his death, according to the ancient logic of the sacred by which only that which has been separated from its past can be brought together for a future act of generation. This is one version of the archaic story that we find wherever the Goddess is worshipped, whether it be in Europe or in India, where the Lady of the Mountain is Parvati, and Siva the lord of the generative moment.

In ancient times the Goddess provided the form of both female and male initiation. Men's societies were active and necessary participants in her worship; from some aspects of it they were, however, barred. In Crete, such initiatory rites were as light-hearted and joyful as they might be sombre and horrifying, as shown in the gaily painted frescoes on the one hand, and in the legends of Dionysiac frenzies – when live bulls were torn apart with hands and teeth alone – on the other. For the foundation rites of the ancient settlements, with their emphasis on an annual sacrifice, were centred on the realization that there is a necessary price to be paid in exchange for reaping the benefits of living together. The wisdom of Goddess-worshipping cultures was to display this necessity as a mystery, rather than a mere spectacle, and to act it out as an individual purgation as well as a universal festivity.

The oldest and most enduring stories of initiation and sacrifice speak of the Goddess as a willing initiate into the mystery of death and regeneration. Inanna's descent into the underworld to meet her dark sister Ereshkigal is perhaps the purest version of the necessity of transformation through death. The same story is best known to us in that of Demeter and Persephone, whose Mysteries at Eleusis in Greece were to be the hope of both men and women until the 4th century AD. When the world itself is threatened with death through the grieving of Demeter for her abducted daughter, Persephone – like Inanna – is able to return to the land of the living in order to prevent the spirit of the Earth from dying through lack of sustenance. Rites of personal regeneration are intimately connected with the continuing fruitfulness of the natural world.

It should come as no surprise, then, to find that the earliest initiation rites should be based around those of women. Women's rites necessarily revolve around their periodicities, and initiation sacralizes the prime moments of puberty and monthly bleeding, of sexual love, birth and motherhood. They also speak of the larger periodicities of Nature and seasonal return, which honour the place of the Goddess in the cosmic cycle. Every initiatory form draws on the metaphor of birth to dramatize the incorporation of the novice into a new status, a new responsibility, a new vision. The female principle, the Goddess, must therefore be present to ensure that the novice goes through the necessary stages of ritual gestation and rebirth.

With the rise of patriarchy, however, men seek to make over the women's rites as their own, forbidding women to witness them on pain of death, in order to isolate the masculine spirit and bring it to an intense self-realization which ultimately increases masculine authority. It is a matter of note how many tribal traditions speak of an original reign of women which the men overthrew. Among the Xinguano Indians of South America, for example, the women initially held possession of the sacred flutes of the tribe, until the

This statue of a pregnant man from Cameroon, West Africa, points to the deep-rooted male envy of woman's ability to procreate.

men tricked them into surrendering them, thus shifting the power to rule into the hands of the men. The Dogon of Africa also tell of a series of thefts: power was stolen from the women by the men, and then the women stole it back again, only to have the men finally wrest it from them once and for all.

Among the Aborigines, the young men's puberty rites involve subincision of the penis in order to mimic menstruation. The psychology of such moments has been diagnosed as womb envy, which the rites are intended to sublimate into a collective ethos. The reality of human sacrifice in the ancient world and the cruel ritual practices of sacrification and general blood-letting recorded in the anthropological world all revolve around issues of power arising from conflict between men and women.

The growing importance of the human victim, both during Maenadic frenzies and in the ritual sacrifice of the king, came to a head in the ancient Mediterranean world with the shift from matriliny to patriliny. The Goddess had long been blamed for her recognition of life's darker aspects, at least from the time of Gilgamesh's taunt, when he was courted by Ishtar, that she had no lover who was not also her victim. This was but speaking the dark truth, but his refusal to accept that inevitable fate only led to disaster. Just as Marduk had warred against Tiamat, Gilgamesh now wars against Ishtar and succeeds in killing her sacred animal, the Bull of Heaven, and her demonized representative Humbaba. Jealous of her power, she retaliates by killing Gilgamesh's companion, Enkidu. This typifies the game of rivalry and revenge that was being played out in real time – for which Ishtar was held to be responsible – in those cruel wars that were waged throughout the Middle East. The price of the change from matriliny to patriliny was now being paid for by outsiders, its cost far over-reaching the ritual sacrifice required in previous times, as the mystery of life was enacted through the profanity of war.

The Greeks who settled in Crete around the 14th century BC were part of a large movement over the Aegean, whose main power was at Mycenae. They were a federation, a tribe of tribes, who swore in the name of their Gods to help each other in the coming war against the Titans, and to defend the rights of monogamous marriage against all-comers. The oath was sworn on the altar of Hecate, Crone Goddess of the Crossroads, and we must suspect that it was made binding by the sacrifice of a daughter, the customary price then paid to the war-Goddess.

This strange custom marks the moment when the mystery rites as practised by men became part of the initiation into warriorhood, during which the Goddess inspired her devotees with battle-frenzy. This inversion of the Goddess's life-affirming energy appears baffling, but when viewed in relation to the institution of monogamous marriage, it begins to make curious sense. To lose in battle, particularly if the men were defending their own territory, was always a bitter humiliation, for it is to the victor that the spoils of war belong, and the women, who were part of the booty, would be raped and possibly impregnated, making it impossible to ensure continued paternity. The Goddess was therefore called upon to drive the men into battle-frenzy in order to satisfy their honour and the need to protect their 'property'. Women were now in the unenviable position of being constantly threatened, requiring the protection of men from other men; as we know, Greek myth tells constantly of rape and revenge. This sets the stage for the

Athene, the motherless maiden, armed for battle as a warrior-Goddess. The snake-haired Gorgon, which represents her destructive aspect, may indicate a link with Anath, worshipped by the Syrians, Egyptians and Canaanites, who was said to hang on her aegis the severed penises of her victims.

Greek miracle of Athene, which represents the third sublimation of the feminine by the masculine. From the head of Olympian Zeus was born a warrior Goddess who, siding with the council of men against the Great Mother Goddess, would transmute men's erstwhile dependence upon her into a mastery of the life-generating principles that were once hers.

The transformation of Athene, a Goddess whose original domain was as wide as that of the Libyan Neith, into a warrior Goddess and mere daughter of Zeus took some generations, and came to a head through a series of rapes and counter-rapes engineered by Zeus' eldest daughter, Ate. A Syrian goddess, later assimilated to Athene, she was known as the one who blinds men to the effect of their actions. Her schemes culminated in the Judgement of Paris, the rape of Helen and the Trojan War. Athene had forsaken her city of Troy to side with the Greeks, and on their victory left Troy for Athens, which thereafter was the city she most favoured. There she sided with Orestes, who had killed his mother, against the avenging Goddesses of matriarchal times, the Furies, thus ensuring what has been called the phallocratic rule of the city and the repression of women. The only escape from their seclusion was when the women gathered together to perform their own ceremonies, such as the Thesmophoria, and when their presence was required to bewail the death of Dionysus, once the Goddess's child, and to celebrate his rebirth. At such times the Maenadic women scoured the wintry mountains to the awe and admiration of the men. No doubt it was their Bacchic fury, primed as much by their social subjection as by the ancient myth, that kept the God alive at the shrine and made it pre-eminent as an oracle until well into Christian times.

Envy and rivalry had characterized Greek politics from the beginning, and interminable wars between the city-states were to bring the Greek era to an end. It was as if Athene, protectress of the city, had joined forces with her *alter ego* Ate to avenge the accumulated injuries done to the female spirit, by making sure that the sins of the fathers would be passed onto their children, along with their patrilineal privileges, to their ultimate undoing.

Upon this Rock

To be fully developed as a human being is to be born male.

Thomas Aquinas

Many of the Gods and Goddesses of Greece found their way to Rome, and though they were known by Roman names, their essential characteristics remained the same: Athene, Aphrodite, Artemis and Hera became Minerva, Venus, Diana and Juno. But one Goddess became the national patroness of Rome and essential to its stability. The Great Mother Goddess Cybele from Phrygia in Asia Minor can be traced back into the early Neolithic. She is not a romanticized, fragmented version of the Goddess but is complete in all her glory, her terror and nurturing power. As a Mountain Goddess, she was conceived as having a vast body, which was the source of all life. Like the wilderness of the mountain she was accompanied by the wilder aspects of Nature; howling wolves, panthers and roaring lions were her companions, the pounding of her drum and the sound of the rattle are the rhythms that she moved to. She was the Mother of the Trojans, and as such began the line from which the first settlers of Rome traced their descent from Troy.

She made her appearance at Rome during the Second Punic War. The Romans, hard-pressed by the Carthaginians, consulted the Sybilline books, which prophesied that 'whenever a foreign enemy has invaded Italy he can

Cybele, Asiatic Mother of the Gods, was a wild and savage deity: 'She is well pleased with the lamentations of castanets, Of kettle-drums and flutes, or the howling of wolves and Sparkle-eyed lions . . .' (Homeric hymn). On the 4th-century silver dish from Parabiago she and her son/lover Attis are shown in a lion-drawn chariot.

only be driven away and vanquished if the Mother of Mount Ida is transferred from Pessinus to Rome'. Soon after, the black meteorite worshipped as the head of the Goddess herself gave voice: 'Let me go. Rome is a worthy residence of any deity'; and once brought to Rome in 205 BC she quickly gave evidence of her power with the defeat of the Carthaginians. First housed in the Temple of Victory, the meteoric head was later transferred to the Phrygianum, near which St Peter's was later built. It is indeed strange to think that the very foundations of the Roman Catholic church may rest upon the head of the most ancient of Earth Mothers.

The Goddess of Asia Minor was a shocking deity to the sensibilities of the Roman authorities. The priests and priestesses who accompanied the ancient Goddess to Rome would stir the people into wild frenzies with their drums, tambourines, ululations and wild dancing. At the height of the ceremony they would become possessed by the deity and flagellate themselves until they bled; following in the footsteps of her castrated son/ lover Attis, the Romans would even castrate themselves voluntarily. Remnants of this ritual survive in Rome even today, where flagellants dedicate themselves to the Virgin Mary during Passion Week. Pre-Christian Rome was very tolerant of the oriental religions and of the Gods and Goddesses of Greece and Egypt. But the ecstatic energy of the cult had not been anticipated, and there were various moves to eliminate it from Rome. Festivals were confined to the Palatine, and Romans were forbidden to be priests of the Goddess until the time of Claudius. In the 4th century AD the Neoplatonists, under Julian, tried valiantly to defend Cybele in terms of her heritage as the Great Mother, and a heated public debate arose between St Augustine, who referred to Attis and his 'harlot mother', and the Neoplatonists together with the Gnostic society of the Nassenes, who upheld the symbolic mystery of Cybele and Attis as the Magna Mater and Sun King. Around AD 400 the Neoplatonist Macrobius declared, 'Who would doubt that the Mother of the Gods should be regarded as the Earth?' But with the triumph of Christianity Attis was banished; the Magna Mater never wholly disappeared, many of Cybele's shrines becoming those of the Mother of God.

The transformation of the old religion's pagan deities and representatives into acceptable Christian saints often carried a high price, a phenomenon best noted in the 5th-century story of Hypatia. At that time the Neoplatonists and Gnostics were viewed as the primary threat to the emerging dogma of the Church of Rome. Hypatia was an initiate of the Eleusinian Mysteries and possibly a priestess of Isis. Head of the Alexandrian library, she is described as the foremost philosopher, mathematician, astronomer and physician of her day. She was well loved by the people and widely known for her public discourses. Bishop Synesius called her 'the Philospher', the most respected of all titles, and other letters sent to her were addressed to the 'Muse' and the 'Oracle'.

In AD 415 Hypatia, while on her way to the library, was apprehended by a group of monks, under the orders of Bishop Cyril, patriarch of Alexandria. She was dragged into the Caesarium, stripped naked and flayed alive with oyster shells, and her remains were burnt. After the death of Hypatia another woman was canonized as Saint Catherine of the Wheel. Her death was equally gruesome, in that she was bound to a 'Catherine Wheel' in

St Catherine of the Wheel, on the point of being saved from her ordeal by a bolt of lightning. She was later beheaded, but angels appeared and carried her body to the top of Mount Sinai. (Martyrdom of St Catherine, altarpiece by Gaudenzio Ferrari, 1484–1546)

order to be simultaneously crushed and burnt. Her popularity as a saint is rivalled only by that of the Virgin Mary herself. However, there is no historical evidence supporting the actual existence of Catherine; furthermore she bears an uncanny resemblance to Hypatia in that she not only lived at the same time and place, but was also known for her ability to outwit her fellow philosophers and for her desire to remain free from marriage. This has led scholars to assume that Hypatia was Christianized and canonized through the fabrication of St Catherine of the Wheel.

We can guess that Hypatia's murder lay heavily upon Cyril's conscience, for his next public move was to appease the feminine principle by raising it to its ancient heights. The opportunity came at the Council of Ephesus, the city once sacred to Diana; there Nestorius objected to the epithet *theotokos*, God-bearer, being bestowed upon the Virgin Mary: 'Let no one call Mary the Mother of God', he had written, 'for Mary was a human being; and that God should be born of a human being is impossible.' Cyril contested this opinion with all the violence for which he was noted, and after an angry hearing, Mary as the God-bearer was formally enshrined at the centre of Christian doctrine.

That Cyril was responsible for the murder of Hypatia and thus for the canonization of St Catherine, as well as for the restoration of the Mother of God, is one of those ironies that characterize the history of the Goddess. We must place Cyril on the same level as Marduk, who killed Tiamat and yet acknowledged Ishtar as 'Star' and war Goddess; or as Orestes, who killed his mother, yet confirmed Athene as the sacred daughter of her father. On all three occasions the exaltation of the Goddess by the patriarchs went hand in hand with the diminishment of women's social standing. One of the philosophical debates of Cyril's time was whether women actually had souls, a question that was part of a wider debate on whether they should continue to take an active part in the church as priestesses. Cyril had already declared the Gnostic Christians to be heretics, because they prayed to a Mother-God as well as a Father-God and allowed women to serve as priestesses, according to a tradition they traced back to Mary Magdalene.

Unbidden Mariolatry

Hail, Holy Queen, Mother of Mercy, our life, our sweetness and our hope, to thee do we pray, poor banished children of Eve . . .

Modern-day Catholic prayer

In spite of the Christian church's initial opposition to the worship of Mary, the needs of the people prevailed – though not without issue. The familiarity and popularity of the divine feminine in the form of Mary presented difficult problems for the Catholic church; initially, they tried to humanize her in order to diminish her divine standing, but, that failing, her virginity and assumption into Heaven would eventually be declared official articles of faith in 1950. The role of the Mother Goddess had long been established in every Western culture, for humanity has always required the presence of a bountiful and merciful deity who would listen to its prayers and offer solace in time of need. Mary became the vehicle by which the old pagan Goddesses could once more take form. The ancients were familiar with virgin Goddesses and saw Mary as part of the Maiden/Mother/Crone triplicity of old: St Bonaventura, in praising Mary, likened her to the old triplicity of Hera, Demeter and Hecate of ancient Greece when he spoke of her being enthroned as Queen of Heaven, as Queen of Earth, where all results from her power, and as Queen of Hell, where she commands respect

The Black Virgin of Montserrat, Spain.
The cult of the Black Virgin spans the Atlantic: both Columbus and Cortés paid their respects to the Black Virgin of Guadalupe before sailing to the New World, and in Mexico an old Aztec site once sacred to the Goddess of Motherhood is now dedicated to Our Lady of Guadalupe.

When an official ruling forbade people to practise the healing arts, women, the traditional herbalists, were easy targets. Here 'three notorious witches' are executed for 'divelish practices' at Chelmsford, Essex, UK, in 1589.

even from the demons. Throughout the Christianized lands the pagan shrines and temples of Diana, Minerva, Artemis, Isis, Hecate, Aphrodite, Tanith and Juno came to be occupied by the Virgin Mary; Notre Dame and other Gothic cathedrals were called 'Palaces of the Queen of Heaven'.

One testimony to the enduring ancient memory of the Prima Mater is thought to be the Black Virgin. These mysterious representations of Mary have been found throughout the Christian world: Clovis, first Christian king of the Franks, reported finding the figure of a Black Virgin in a forest glen, protected by a lioness and her cubs, and at Chartres her image was discovered in a grotto beneath the cathedral. As far back as AD 44 the cult of the Black Virgin was well established in France, and she has continued to be worshipped in Spain, Poland, Switzerland, Italy, England and the New World down to the present day. The fact that these images of Mary are black has either been overlooked or dismissed as an accident caused by the smoke of candles or incense. But they are also thought to express an echo of the rites of Black Isis and Diana, Cybele and Persephone, Inanna and Lilith. Symbolically, the Black Virgin is interpreted as the waiting, fertile black Earth or the deepest recesses of a cave, womb-like and unrevealed; psychologically, she occupies the underworld and is the stuff from which the soul is made. Her sublimated message is one that asks us to confront the Goddess as Nature and Nature as feminine. Yes, she is abundant, fertile and capable of giving birth, but like her black sister Kali she can devour her children and dance upon the bodies of the dead.

Throughout the Dark and Middle Ages the Virgin Mary was venerated as protectress. The lifestyle of the people and the closeness with which they lived to the Earth required that they keep alive many of the ancient Earth-renewal ceremonies: spring was a time for planting and fertility ceremonies, blessing of the fields and May-pole dances; autumn was the time of harvest home and the Day of the Dead. All of this seasonal ritual activity was recognized as forming part of the cycle of the Earth Mother, and it was officially sanctioned by the Christian church – for the church fathers were quick to adopt the old pagan calendar of festivals and transform them into Christian feast days.

The sacred groves of the past were now replaced by cathedrals, but as these grew more grandiose, frequent sightings of the 'White Lady' were reported. Her place had always been in Nature, and it was to the sacred sites that she returned, calling her people to her. The Goddess as living Nature continued to thrive amongst the peasant peoples of the world, and the springs and wells that she frequented became the inspiration for large pilgrimages that criss-crossed Europe. These holy places of Nature were the abode of the Goddess known as Brigit, Morgan, Helen, Notre Dame, Mary and Hel-Eve, to name a few, and they were the source of miraculous healings now dedicated to the Virgin.

The people of Europe had never given up 'the old ways', and women in particular had kept the folk-magic tradition alive through the making of charms, the wearing of laurels, by offering food to the spirit of the hearth and bread to the holy wells. Though the women were no longer able to be priestesses, many still served the community as mid-wives and healers. But soon the power of these wise women came to be perceived as a threat. In the 13th century the first witch trials began, and they continued until the

19th century. Over the years tens of thousands, if not millions of people lost their lives to the Inquisitors or reformers. It is one of the unspoken holocausts of our age. Entire villages in Switzerland were destroyed, with a total of 7000 women burned in two villages alone; 5000 people were executed in Strasbourg over a twenty-year reign of terror; Geneva burned 500 witches in three months, and Toulouse 400 in a day. The wise women of the past, who would once have been Sybils and prophetesses, were now tortured and murdered as creatures of darkness.

Nature, Woman and the Goddess

Whatever befalls the Earth befalls the sons of the Earth.
Man does not weave the web of life, he is merely a strand in it.
Whatever he does to the web he does to himself

Chief Seattle

The shrine of Our Lady of Walsingham is the primary pilgrimage centre of the Black Virgin in England. In 1989 10,000 people attended her feast-day procession, at which a small but vocal group of fundamentalist Christians demonstrated an enduring intolerance within the Anglican church towards the Queen of Heaven.

The fates of woman, Nature and the Goddess are inextricably linked. The same zealous mistrust and fear that were projected towards women as witches would now be directed to the whole of Nature. As Francis Bacon said in the 16th century, 'We will place Nature on the rack and torture her secrets out of her.' The great mystery of the Goddess came under the anatomizing eye of the rational God of science. The old world view had perceived the Earth as a living body, a living being, who since the beginning of time had been acknowledged as the Earth Mother. The power of life did not originate from a transcendent outside force, but was rather an immanent power contained within the field of Nature. To Christianity this view was, of course, heresy, and the Protestant Reformation was determined to break away from all the old pagan and Goddess-tinged activities of the past. God as the Creator had to be firmly established as existing outside the field of Nature and the body of the Goddess. He and his heavenly realm had to be presented as the only refuge from the tempting, dangerous and sinful world of Nature. This reductionist perspective denied the oneness of all creation and offered in its place a dualistic view that split matter and spirit, feminine and masculine, life and death, good and evil.

Early scientists, such as Giordano Bruno, Isaac Newton, Nicolas Copernicus, and Johannes Kepler – whose mother was almost burnt as a witch – had all found their inspiration in Nature and constructed their reasoning through the old traditions of nature-magic and alchemy. But the Reformation spoke against anything remotely connected with magic or folk tradition. The scientists of the 16th and 17th centuries were therefore faced with the task of finding a new language in which to explain the natural order and the habits of Nature. They adopted a mechanistic view, a philosophical position that would not conflict with Christian doctrine, for if the Earth and the universe are a huge machine, then somewhere behind the curtain is the machine-maker, God. More important was the implication that the Earth and her creatures, as part of this machine, are insensate, predictable and controllable, and that since mankind is made in the image of God, scientists are authorized mechanics who can tinker with Nature in whatever way they choose. Mechanism represents the fourth sublimation of the feminine by the masculine mind, in that the living world or body of Gaia becomes an abstract idea rather than the actual matrix in which all life participates.

The unholy alliance that was formed between the newly developing Age of Reason and Christianity would permit the wholesale slaughter of Nature. The discovery of the New World is testimony to the ambivalent sense of wonder, fear and loathing with which Nature in her wild and prolific state was viewed. The careless cutting of the hardwood forest that once reached unbroken from the east coast of North America to the Mississippi river, and the slaughter of the great buffalo herds reveal the true quality of the European mind as it encountered Nature as she should be, as she had once been in their own native lands. The American Indians, romantically conceived as 'noble savages', reminded the Europeans of a paradise lost, yet the Indians too would be exterminated, in spite of their repeated protestations that they could no more sell their land than sell the clouds that drift in the sky, that the Earth was and is their Mother, the sky their Father. Unfortunately, the pioneering spirit of the settlers had been fanned too bright; Nature was theirs for the taking, and the religion and science of the day affirmed their rights both to conquer and to exercise dominion over all the creatures of the Earth.

A Gaian View

It is lovely indeed, it is lovely
indeed . . .
I, I am the spirit within the Earth;
The bodily strength of the Earth is
my strength;
The thoughts of the Earth are my
thoughts;
All that belongs to the Earth belongs
to me;
I, I am the sacred words of the Earth;
It is lovely indeed, it is lovely
indeed . . .

Navaho Creation Chant of
Changing Woman

Two hundred years after the Enlightenment science finds itself, like the Great Goddess of old, parcelled out into its constituent parts, each discipline holding its own place on Mount Olympus. The fundamental units of Nature have been broken down into separate fields of study as her mysteries have been slowly tortured out of her. Today, faced with what appears to be an inevitable catastrophic environmental disaster, science is finding itself required to break down the barriers between the various disciplines in order to understand the full complexity of the living planetary system. As a result, the old mechanistic, reductionist world view that started with the Greeks has begun to crumble. We can no longer afford to look at life as if we were outsiders; instead, we must see humanity as just one participant in a field of rich diversity that is continuously shifting and changing. Humankind must place itself once more in the context of the greater fabric of life.

Yet scientists continue to speak of 'matter' as if it were dead, lacking in emotional response, there to be dissected and examined, while faith in the cleverness of our technological advances continues to override the wisdom of Nature. Breakthroughs in genetic engineering and *in vitro* fertilization hearken back to the ancient Greeks, who viewed the female as an incubator for the life-generating male seed. The unwinding of the Goddess' DNA serpent, emerging 'birth technologies' and the creation of life in a test tube form the fifth and final sublimation of the female by the masculine energy. It is as if the entire thrust of our psychological history has been subconsciously directed towards unravelling the mystery of the Great Goddess and taking over her life-producing ability. Having begun with what Joseph Campbell labelled the 'patriarchal inversion' of the initial creation myths, the masculine mind is now on the verge of usurping birth itself.

Some scientists, however, in confronting the urgency of the environmental problem, are now calling our planet by the name of Gaia, after the Greek Earth Goddess known as the 'Oldest of the Divinities'. The Gaia Hypothesis recognizes that the Earth is a self-regulating system, a macro-organism that has co-operation and mutualism at its core. The synergy inherent in the Earth and its multitude of macro- and micro-systems maintains itself through a series of nested morphogenetic fields. The success or demise of one system or species has far-reaching and interpenetrating consequences for the entire 'nest'. Complex living things always have order and wholeness as a feature of their existence, and Gaia is no exception.

The sense of harmonious well-being that results when the male and female forces are in balance is epitomized in Japanese carvings of the male-female deity, Dosojin.

What Gaia brings to our attention is the epistemological error that began back in the Near East, when the myth of monotheism was invented, and when the Goddess and animism were banished. We can trace the continuous thread of this alien mode of thought through history, discovering how it has affected our relationships with Nature and with one another. It becomes ever more obvious that the Earth and life itself is not a machine, a steam engine or a computer; that competition is not the primary ordering principle in Nature, and that co-operation is a far more stable and successful solution. One cannot help remembering the cultures of Çatal Hüyük, Hacilar or Mohenjo-daro, which survived prosperously and harmoniously until they were overthrown by the ancestors of our present civilization. Humanity is descended, it seems, from a split heritage: the one peaceful and stable, the other competitive and wildly fluctuating. The impulse must now be to validate those cultures that model harmonious, stable relationships.

As tidings of ill-omen spread, nuclear disaster, over-population, toxic waste, holes in the ozone layer, the 'greenhouse effect' and a new Ice Age are but a few of the very real problems facing us and future generations. The great irony of this moment of possible annihilation and the simultaneous recognition of Gaia reminds us of the ancient Greeks and the fall of Troy. As a child, Cassandra, daughter of King Priam of Troy, was found asleep in the temple with two snakes licking her ears, a sure sign that the gift of prophecy had been bestowed upon her. As the princess grew, Apollo desired her for one of his priestesses and demanded that she speak the truth as Zeus knew it, not as the Goddess did. Cassandra allowed him but one kiss, and in revenge he spat into her mouth, making certain that no one would believe her from that moment on. As a result, the Prophetess was driven mad by the fact that the doom she foretold for Troy could not be averted. With the fall of that symbolic city the old Goddess-worshipping cultures came to an end, and Cassandra's name has ever since been given to women who interrupt men's counsels to warn them of the consequences of their actions. We can no longer afford to turn a deaf ear to the fate of the Earth, for too many ordinary women and men have had their ears licked by the Goddess's snakes. The truthful voice of Cassandra will be heard this time.

In the not so distant past the Goddess as Nature was an integral part of life. Today, for some she is an admirable folk tale, for others an archetypal ideal symbolic of wholeness; and for a few she is a metaphysical reality and source of renewal, strength and blessing. The synchronicity of her again being called Gaia reminds us of our true heritage as children of the Earth – but let us not forget that she is also known as Kali, the one who devours her children. The forgotten knowledge of the past is a carnal or sensual knowledge that must be redeemed and sanctified. The very idea of sanctification, or *sanctitas*, returns us to the Tellurian Mother of the ancient past. Bachofen made a fine distinction between *sacrum*, that which is made sacred by being dedicated by men to the gods above, and *sanctum*, that which from the beginning is under the protection of the feminine chthonic powers. For him, sanctity is the equivalent of 'Earth-Godliness', the relationship any object or living thing has with the maternal womb of the Earth, the inner sanctum or 'untouchable place'. Integrating *sanctitas* into our world view may be of the utmost importance for the continuation of the human species.

In the end, it is to the Taoists that we must turn, for embedded in their timeless wisdom is the poetry of the Goddess and the story of the feminine spirit. Their acute observation and understanding of Nature as feminine emphasized all that was mystical and receptive; its yielding quality was adopted as the model on which correct social relations should be based. And yet the very concept of Yin was based upon Yang, a word meaning 'to give up the better place, to invite'. Accordingly, the prestige of a man was dependent upon his ability to yield or give away to his peoples whatever was required. This 'liquidization' of masculine aggressiveness is thought to be essential in creating a co-operative social organization. The recognition of the receptive passivity of water and the feminine teaches the Taoist principle of leadership from within, for moving water can wear away the hardest of substances, and in so doing, water running through valleys constantly cleanses and renews itself. The transformation in consciousness that is required for the new millennium is not simply a return to the old matriarchal ways, but involves an entirely new way of participating fully in life. It is only the combination of the two forces of the feminine and the masculine, working in harmony as a united 'soft' power, that can bring about radical change. The old model of hard power is about domination and control, power over others, places and things; it generates fear and alienation and is often enforced with violence. Soft power comes from within and generates a sense of connection and creativity. It is the power of mutual respect and vision; as such, it is empowering and capable of spontaneous rapid growth and transformative change. The reintegration of this wisdom and the Beauty Way of the life-affirming feminine is essential for the survival of future generations and of Gaia herself. The Goddess returns to us at this time as a reminder of who we are, where we come from and where we are going. Through her we may find ourselves once again living in a sacred context. The Taoist exaltation of the restorative powers of the Goddess and Nature is best expressed in the *Tao te Ching*:

> The Valley Spirit never dies.
> It is named the Mysterious Feminine.
> And the doorway of the Mysterious Feminine
> Is the base from which Heaven and Earth sprang.
> It is there within us all the while.
> Draw upon it as you will, it never runs dry.

Nine dancing apsaras from a temple frieze in Indonesia (12th–13th c.) express the ecstatic energy of the female spirit.

With her coiled black hair, winged shoulders and smiling reptilian face, this Babylonian Goddess presents an ancient and haunting image of the sacred mother. Holding her child to her breast, she stands upright like Tiamat, the dragon woman, naked except for her magic belt of triangles, which serves to emphasize as well as beautify her own fertile delta. The triangle represents the triple aspect of the Great Goddess as Maiden, Mother and Crone, and is recognized in the Tantric tradition as the primary symbol of life. The serpent force is the great life-affirming, maternal blessing. The snake is always associated with immortality, for every year it has the gift of shedding its old skin and emerging renewed and reborn, while the woman sheds her inner skin once a month. (Ur, 4000–3500 BC, terracotta, h.15cm, $5\frac{3}{4}''$)

How the one Great Goddess became the many is inherent in the nature of time and its passing. For although she is one, she is also like a multi-faceted jewel that sparkles in every direction and reflects all that it sees. As the nine-fold Muse (*right*) she has been the source of inspiration for humanity. The Mistress of Incantations was first known as Mnemosyne, or Memory, the one who taught the stories of old to the bards. The Muses are now known as Thalia (comedy), Terpsichore (dance), Clio (history), Euterpe (lyric poetry and music), Polymnia (sacred song), Erato (love poetry), Urania (astronomy), Calliope (epic poetry) and Melpomene (tragedy). (Trier, West Germany, 2nd century, Roman mosaic)

The ten Mahāvidyās, or Great Wisdoms (*above*), are a reminder of how the dark forces and the pure light combine to keep the wheel of life turning. The ascending and descending realities circle endlessly, while the transformation of the Goddess – from Kali, the primary evolutionary principle, through Tara, the force for spiritual ascent, and Tripura Bhairavi, the destroyer, and finally to Kamala, the one who embodies good fortune and unity – speaks of her liberating and unifying yet paradoxical nature. The Tantric tradition emphasizes that 'life and its manifold processes are not an inert, even state of oneness; what justifies existence is variety, contradiction, change and multiplicity.' (Madhu Khanna) (Mithila, India, 20th century, watercolour on paper)

The face of this New Guinea woman (*right*), with its predominance of red, the cowrie-shell necklace, and the crescent-moon-shaped shell on the forehead, takes us back to the Paleolithic caves, where cowries and red ochre, representing the female and her blood mysteries, were found in abundance. The impulse to adorn and beautify the body is extremely ancient. The very word 'cosmetic' is a derivative from the Greek *kosmetikos*, meaning a sense of harmony and order, or one skilled in adorning.

The cosmic patterns on the Mexican pregnant pot (*above*) are part of a long tradition in the Americas. The geometric four-step pattern on her body tells of the different ages or worlds of the past and the future; creation is said to be now leaving the fourth world and entering the fifth. The diamond shape on her belly is the Morning Star, and on her face are quadrants honouring the four directions. All of these patterns are still being woven into the textiles of the present-day native population. (Michoacán, Mexico: Chupicuaro culture, 600–100 BC, terracotta, h.30 cm, 11¾")

These two representatives of the Goddess – one from Mesopotamia (*right*: 4th century BC), the other from the Congo (*left*: Ouroua tribe, 19th–20th century) – offer their breasts to the world in a timeless sacred gesture, a reminder to all that it is through the breast that life is nurtured. Both figures gaze directly towards us with expressions of beneficent knowing. The elixir of life they offer to all is the milk of wisdom. On their bodies are diamond-shaped motifs that emphasize the navel and the pubic triangle. Diamond itself means 'world Goddess', and its first syllables mean 'the shining one', as in 'Diana' and 'divine'. The purity and hardness of the diamond are associated with divine essence and, in Tibet, with the great Wisdom Goddess Tara. The navel, or omphalos, is the centre of the world, and represents the Goddess as the source of all life, the centre from which all things arise.

The mystery of the generations is first contained within the body of the mother. In the entrance of a cave our ancestors of the Upper Paleolithic carved an image of the Great Mother, who announced to all that she was with child. The Venus of Laussel (*left*) is ample, naked and faceless; her pendulous breasts, belly and pubic triangle are clearly marked. In one hand she appears to hold the moon in the form of a bison horn stained with red ochre; thirteen notches have been carved upon it. Her other hand points to her pregnant belly, telling the simple facts of life: conception takes place on the fourteenth day after a woman's moon-time. Twenty thousand years later, another annunciation would be proclaimed. Like that of the Great Goddess of old this announcement is made inside a cave-like room evoking the womb of the maternal being. In Piero della Francesca's *Madonna del Parto* (*right*: c. 1460, fresco), two angels stand at the entrance, parting the curtains of the cave to reveal a solemn Virgin Mary who indicates the root of the deepest of all Christian mysteries. Unlike the Venus of Laussel, this mother-to-be is heavily clothed; her pregnant belly is not shown except through a slit in her robe. The mystery told here has nothing to do with the moon, blood or men, for this is an immaculate conception, unstained by the sexual act. As a consequence it is inconceivable — that is, a miracle.

42

There is perhaps no other time at which mortal woman is closer to the sacred feminine than in the act of giving birth. It is, after all, the process of birth and death that sustains the Great Mother, and birth always contains the seed of death. The power of the Goddess is witnessed in these women who stand upright to push new life into the world. The pre-historic Sabaean rock painting from the Yemen (*above*) shows a mirror image of mother and child, connected by the umbilicus; the lines of energy radiating from the child's head exemplify the continuing stream of life. The 18th century wood carving from southern India (*left*) depicts the calm delight that can come to a woman who has made herself one with the Goddess. Her three attendants reflect her composure, their task being simply to ease the baby gently into existence. The mystery of transformation is revealed to the woman through the growth of the foetus and the moment of birth, and this most ancient of blood mysteries, which opens all women to true communion with each other, is the very foundation of human social life.

The primordial mysteries of the feminine have always been associated with vegetation, through women's intimacy with the plant world. Flowers, fruit, maize and wheat are not only a source of nourishment, but also symbols of fertility. The blossoming of the maiden is characterized by the flowers that she carries, her maturity by the fruit that she bears. The buds that will open are the unfolding of the mysteries of love and life, in which the womb transforms itself through the act of conception and generation. The young maiden bedecked with flowers personifies the principles of fertility and growth; in French 'les fleurs' is another name for a young girl's first blood. It is the West Wind as the breath of Spring that transforms Chloris, the Green One, into Flora, the Primavera (*right*), while among the Aztecs Xochiquetzal, the Goddess of flowers and love, is associated with festivities of spring and sacred dance; joyous song issues from her mouth in flowery scrolls (*below*). It is from the flower or the fruit of life that the elixir of immortality is drawn. (detail: Sandro Botticelli, *Primavera*, c. 1482, tempera on panel; detail: *Codex Borbonicus*, early 16th-century Aztec religious calendar)

She has been called the Lady of the
Beasts and Mistress of Animals; her
names in Europe and Egypt include
Artemis, Hecate, Cybele, Hathor,
Isis, Britomartis, Dictynna, Circe,
Leto and Lilith. Wherever she is
found she appears as a 'virgin', a
woman who is one in and of
herself. On the Boeotian amphora
(*above*) we see her with winged
arms gathering the animals towards
her, while in the tapestry (*right*) her
pavilion is held open by the lion
and the unicorn as a shelter for the
beasts in her charge. Animals both
wild and domestic, of the sky, land
and sea pay homage to her and
she in turn to them, for she unites
all pairs of opposites. This mutuality
is representative of a participation
mystique, in which all living
creatures are recognized as being
interdependent. As the Lady of the
Beasts, the Goddess is responsible
for the hunt, and it is to her that
the hunters make their offerings
and to the spirits of the animals
that they give their thanks. (Athens,
geometric amphora, *c.* 680 BC;
Cluny, France, *The Lady and the
Unicorn* tapestry, late 15th century)

The transformative power of the Goddess – her ability to take on the shape of animals in general, and of birds and snakes in particular – is one of her many gifts. The soaring of birds between the Earth and the Sky realm is indicative of the soul-flight of the shaman and the visionary message that is returned to the people. The ancient Saharan rock painting of four Bird-Goddesses, representing the black, yellow, red and white races, also speaks of the shaman's ecstatic journey to the world beyond (*below*). Standing at the four cardinal points, wearing serpents on their heads, and with arms upraised, they invoke the powers of Heaven and Earth.

(Jabbaren, 3500–2500 BC) In *Blue Hummingbird Holding Earth and Sky* (*left*), by contemporary artist Colleen Kelley (1986, oil on canvas), the Hummingbird Goddess stands open to the world. She is inside a *kiva*, or underground temple; behind her are the ancestors, and in her hand she holds the feathered serpent known in Mexico as Quetzalcoatl. According to legend, a blue hummingbird messenger was said to have led the drought-stricken inhabitants of Chaco Canyon to a new home near a sacred lake in Mexico. Her message is one of immanence, as she looks toward the 'sky window' and to Nature beyond.

The Great Goddess is the Sacred Mountain. It is here, in the lap of the Goddess, that the *hieros gamos* between Heaven and Earth takes place. The Mountain Mother visibly rules over the land around her, and places such as Machu Picchu, Annapurna, Chomo-Lung-Ma (Mount Everest), Mount Hara and Mount Fuji remind us that they are the Goddess enthroned in Nature. The image of Sacred Purity rising out of the mountain peak, flanked by her guardian lions (*right*), is reminiscent of the ancient Mountain Goddess Cybele of Anatolia. Likewise, the representative of the Goddess from Sumeria sits enveloped in ceremonial robes, upon her mountain throne (*left*). The name of the great queen 'Isis' literally means 'throne', and kings everywhere come into their full power by returning to the lap of the Goddess through the act of 'mounting the throne'. (Workshop of Hans Memling, *Sacred Purity*, 15th century; Mari, seated Goddess, c. 2400 BC)

In Bali the dark aspect of the feminine is personified by the evil witch/widow Rangda (*right*). The ceremony dedicated to her and the good dragon Barong is conducted at a crossroads, the haunt of the dark Goddess of Fate known as Hecate in ancient Greece. Like Shiva's wife Durga, Rangda is never eliminated, for she is the great destroyer and bringer of death. In the Balinese dance-pantomime, which is also a form of exorcism, the men fall under the spell of Rangda and try to impale themselves on their sharp *kris*, or daggers. It is Barong who temporarily banishes Rangda and saves men by sprinkling them with holy water. The gruesome persistence of Rangda reveals the Goddess in her most profound relationship to life and death, for she is the one who opens and closes wombs.

When the Great Demon Mahisasura, representing the destructive forces of the phallic principle, threatened the world with his ignorance, the Great Goddess Durga let out her battle cry (*above*). Seated on her tiger, she confronted his vast battalion of demons with an army of ferocious Goddesses, created out of her own breath, including Parvati, Kalika and Ambika. In her blackest rage, the Goddess gave birth to a terrifying and emaciated Kali, who let out the deafening sacred syllable of *Hum* and slew the demons' army. Kali then drank the *rakta-bija*, or seed-blood, of the demons to neutralize the destructive power of the masculine energy. (Kangra School, India, c. 18th century, gouache on paper)

The Lady of Wild Things is the Goddess in her untamed manifestation. She is one with all aspects of Nature, from howling wolves to gentle deer. She strides through the wilderness unfettered by civilization, filled with an orgiastic passion for life. As Wild Woman, she is fearless, and when she rages as a Maenad she is known to strike terror into the hearts of the strongest men. Here, on a Greek vase of the early 5th century BC, a fawn skin is draped over her shoulder; a snake coils around her arm; her feet are bare upon the Earth (right). A Tassili rock painting from Saharan Africa, the 'White Lady' of Aouanrhet, shows her running, naked except for a loin cloth and what must be the beauty marks of scarification from her puberty rite (left). The ecstatic spirit of these wild maidens would later become part of the sacred mysteries of Dionysus, and of Demeter at Eleusis.

The fortune of the world is regulated by a Goddess who wears the face of the moon, undergoing her changes as an example to women. In ancient Rome she was known as Fortuna, whose emblem in the West is the wheel of luck, on which women and men can rise to fortune – and hence fall. Some have called her fickle because of her capacity for change. In India she is Lakshmi, born like Aphrodite from the sea of the world's beginnings; and in Japan she is Kichijo-ten, who carries in her hand the wish-bestowing jewel that is the world itself (*left*). As Moon Mother, she is sometimes called Chance, and in this form she steers the life of the universe through the waters of time (*above*). (Japan, Nara period: 8th century, colour on hemp; Annie Truxell, *Journey to Mu*, 1986, ink and acrylic)

The image of the Cosmic Woman illustrates that all things are born of woman – even the gods. She sits with arms upraised, radiating outwards, while Brahma the Creator rests in her yoni. Between her breasts, Vishnu the Preserver maintains the world, and on her crown sits Shiva, the Lord of the Universe. All their power is impotent without the creative energy of the Goddess as Śakti, for she alone provides the inner force of all outward manifestations. (Rajasthan, India, 18th century, gouache on paper)

The Holy Mother Church also recognizes this principle. The carved shrine of the Virgin (*right*) opens up to reveal that the sacred mysteries of the Church, along with God the Father and God the Son, are contained within the body of the Virgin. The worship of the most merciful Mary clearly reaches back to our pagan roots, where she was exalted as the Queen of Heaven. Like this carved shrine, the great cathedrals, which were often dedicated to 'Notre Dame', serve to remind us that when we enter them, we are entering the body of the Mother of God. (Germany, late 13th to early 14th century, wood covered with linen, gesso and gilt)

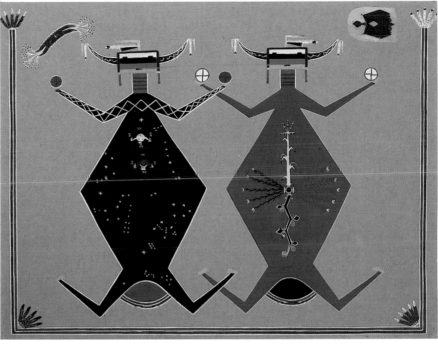

The cosmic union of the masculine and the feminine forces is the sacred marriage rite. This unification of opposites gives birth to the phenomenal world, whether it be in India, with Shiva and Śakti, or in Japan, where the Wedded Rocks at Futamigaura personify the legendary creators of Japan, Izanagi and Izanami. Among the Navajo Indians the cosmic couple are simply called Earth Mother and Sky Father (*above*): she contains the maize within her body and he, the firmament. In sand paintings they are always of equal size and importance, for nothing is possible without this harmonious primal relationship; the Beauty Way Chant of the Navajo prays equally to both forces:

'Earth by which it is long life by
    that I am long life as I say this.
Sky by which it is long life by
    that I am long life as I say this.
It has become blessed again, it
    has become blessed again.
It has become blessed again, it
    has become blessed again.'

It is the radiant and benevolent nature of the Lady of Angels and the Lotus Goddess of Supreme Wisdom that draws one towards transformation and illumination. Transported off the Earth either by her lotus boat or the crescent moon, she rises into the cosmic heavens, her spiritual essence encircled in light. She bestows 'perfection of knowledge', and through the virtue of her divine womanhood represents the purest form of spiritual transformation. Tara stands upon the lotus, primary symbol of the yoni (*left*). In the West the sacred flower of the Virgin Goddess became the self-fertilizing lily or fleur-de-lis, symbol of Lilith, Astarte, Juno and Mary. Those who offer themselves to the serene Goddess of Purity become 'like lotus blossoms that rise from the water's surface and open their petals to the unbroken light of heaven' (Heinrich Zimmer). (France, *Virgin and Virtues*, 16th–17th century, enamel plaque; Tibet, *Tara*, 18th century, gouache and gold on cloth)

At the centre of the Huichol cosmology is the ingesting of the peyote cactus by the tribe. The visionary realm that is illuminated within is said to aid the people in finding their lives. To the Huichols, all of Nature is imbued with spirits.

Great-Grandmother Nakawe holds within her body the dove, who personifies Our Mother Kukuruku, the spirit of the maize. When the Earth has been made fertile by the sun above her head and the Rain Goddesses of the four directions, then the maize plants grow out of the body of Tatei (Our Mother) Urianaka. (Crescencio Perez Robles, *Goddess of the Earth Ready for Planting*, 20th century, yarn on plywood, beeswax)

Gate of Initiation

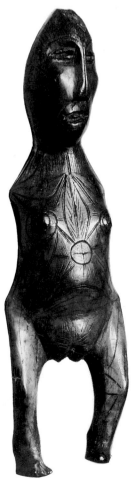

The first rite of passage of all human beings begins in the womb and ends between the thighs of the Great Mother. In India, the vagina, known as the yoni, is also called cunti or kunda, the root-word of 'cunning', 'cunt' and 'kin'. Throughout the ancient world the yoni was worshipped as an object of great mystery: the entrance to caves, enclosures with gates and pillars, all represent the womb sanctuary of the divine feminine. (Megalithic dolmen, Malabar, India) Yet the place of birth and the place where the dead were laid to rest were often one and the same. In Malekula (Melanesia) the word for a dolmen means to 'come out from, or to be born'. These womb-like tomb structures of stone were either natural configurations, or enclosures constructed in such a way as to remind people of the body of the Great Mother. It was here that the mystery of birth and rebirth was enacted.

Countless images, from every age and every culture, honour the Mount of Venus without a hint of shame.

(Eskimo fertility figure of walrus ivory, Okuik culture, Alaska, 1st c. BC) In the Tantric tradition of India the yoni is displayed in temples for all to honour and respect as a source of life, beauty and pleasure. (Icon of the Goddess as genetrix, Hyderabad, c.600: *opposite, above left*) If the carving is in reach of its admirers, the yoni will often be polished to a shine by the touching of fingers wishing to invoke the blessings of the Goddess. The bronze yoni water pot (South India, 18th c.: *opposite, below left*) is another elegant example of how the life force flows through the feminine.

This open delight in the vulva is somewhat foreign to western culture, but not unknown. In Celtic Britain there are churches that still contain remnants of the old pagan ways which celebrated the body of woman. The Sheela-na-Gig is one such reminder. (Church of St Mary and St David, Kilpeck, Herefordshire, UK: *opposite, above right*) But her message is double-edged: the opening of her vagina and the smile on her face elicit both awe and terror; one might venture too far inside her and never return to the light

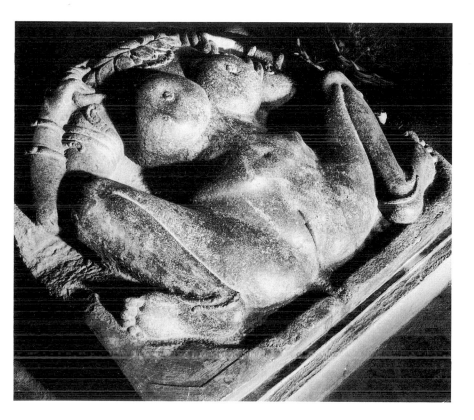

of day again. The stone stele from Cerro Jaboncillo in Ecuador highlights the yoni in such a way as to reveal the *mons Veneris* as the place where three roads meet. The crossroads is always a symbol of the Triple Goddess, and of the old crone in particular. It is here that offerings are made to the Dark Goddess of life and death, for it is the best place to perform acts of magic.

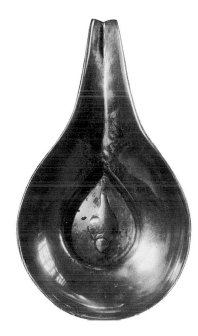

A Labour of Love

Tantric traditions recognize that every woman is a representative of the divine principle known as Śakti. Through the arousal of the *kundalini* force, each woman can ascend to her highest creative potential, for the cosmic insemination of snake power awakens in the woman an ultimate awareness of reality. This act of awakening and the projection of this force into the world at large are most commonly manifested through the process of giving birth. The leonine pregnant woman from Phoenicia personifies the period of incubation required in order to bring something beautiful into the world. (Cemetery at Akhziv, Israel, 5th c. BC) Her introspective mood speaks to us of the hidden reservoirs of strength, serenity and wisdom that can be

awakened by stepping into the unknown.

The act of giving birth, whether to a child, an idea or a piece of art, is never without its pain. The Huichol Indians believe that the woman's partner should share in both the pain and the pleasure of giving birth, so, while she labours, her husband sits in the rafters above her with a rope tied to his testicles. Every time she has a contraction she tugs upon the rope. In the end, he is just as joyous at the birth of the child as she is – possibly more so! This sharing of the birth pangs, known as couvade, where the husband maintains a sympathetic brooding around the arrival of the child, is common among many native peoples. (Contemporary Huichol yarn painting, California, USA)

Like most important moments in life, birth is best approached on one's feet. These scenes of birth from three

different continents all show women in the squatting position as they deliver the child. (Aztec stone sculpture of Tlacolteutl, goddess of childbirth, Aplite, Valley of Mexico, 1325–1521; bronze needle head, Luristan, 1st millennium BC; Aboriginal rock painting, Anbangbang shelter, Kunwinjke Bim, Western Arnhem Land, Australia) They may have attendants nearby, but it is the force of gravity that aids the women in delivering the child. The miracle of birth was and should still be a moment of empowerment for all women, as it is deeply connected with the mystery of transformation. The transformative nature of the feminine 'as "creative principle" encompasses the whole world. This is the totality of Nature in its original unity, from which all life arises and unfolds, assuming, in its highest transformation, the form of the spirit' (Erich Neumann).

The Milk of Loving Kindness

According to the Greeks, the first bowl was shaped from the breast of Helen of Troy, and even today Zuni women of North America make their pottery in the shape of the breast. (Pot of East European Lausitz culture, c.1400–500 BC) The rhyton from Mochlos in Crete (c.2000 BC) and the Post-Classic Mexican pitcher from Huastec (*below left* and *right*) are sacred vessels which played an important role in the ritual life of the people. The pouring forth of milk from the breasts represents a continuation of the mysteries of transformation, and is a reminder of the generous nature of the Goddess; when she is viewed as a vessel, her abilities to nurture, provide, contain and protect, as well as to gather all back into her womb, are honoured.

In Java an 11th-century image of the Goddess Belahan is carved into the side of a bathing pool, so that the water of the sacred spring can flow through the breasts and then into the pool (*opposite, right*). In this way the spring is recognized as the domain of the Goddess, while the act of bathing becomes a rite of purification and healing – for pure water is the next best thing to mother's milk.

The holding and offering of the breasts is part of the epiphany of the Goddess, whereby she reminds us that through her all life is sustained. When Demeter mourned the loss of her daughter Persephone, the entire world became barren, and the gods were forced to plead with her to restore the bounty of the Earth. (Greek terracotta, 5th c. BC: *opposite, above right*) Even in death the four representatives of the Goddess Astarte offer their breasts to nourish the soul on its passing into the underworld and beyond, and to reaffirm that death as well as life is under the protection of the Goddess. (End panel of limestone sarcophagus, Amathus, Cyprus, 6th c. BC)

Gaia Genetrix

The blood mysteries of the feminine begin with the first menstruation, when the girl's body is transformed into that of a woman. With pregnancy, it is again the blood that feeds the growing foetus inside the mother, and at birth it

is blood that seemingly transforms itself into life-giving milk. The image of the mother with her child is the most persistent and universal of themes: we find her carved in stone in caves from the Paleolithic, as highly stylized, incised figures from Eastern Europe and the Mediterranean, even in the more recent sculpture of Henry Moore. (Geometric figure, Cyprus, 2300–2000 BC; Henry Moore, bronze *Mother and Child*, 1953)

Generally, she is shown with one child at her breast, but there are also images of her more bountiful nature, where she is nursing twins. In many cultures the arrival of twins is thought to be a most inauspicious moment, and they are promptly despatched. Many

In Egypt Queen Isis, known as the Lady of Abundance, offers her breast to an almost grown Horus, perhaps to remind him of where the source of his power is located. (Temple entrance carving, Dendera) The communion that Isis offered the world was one of bread, which she made possible by discovering the corn, and of milk, which flowed from her breasts. The initiate drank the milk from a cup that was modelled in the shape of a woman's breast, thus remembering that Isis as Mother Nature was mother to all.

The Yoruba woman with her child at the breast (Nigerian wooden sculpture, 19th–20th c.) and the Peruvian effigy contrast the realities of motherhood. The queenly African carries her motherhood proudly as she sits with her child, who suckles her huge and erect breasts. The Peruvian woman, however, carries her child turned away from her breast. (Early Peruvian vase from the Moche Valley near Trujillo) Around her head she wears the strap that is used for carrying heavy loads, her body bent under the weight of such a load. The biological imperative towards motherhood can in reality be a burden as well as a blessing.

dualistic systems are based on the arrival of twins. Often, as in Christianity, one is God and the other is his twin brother the devil; in Persia the same holds true for the birth of Mazda and Ahriman; while the Celtic Goddess Arianrhod gave birth to the twins Dylan and Lleu, who were the dual powers of light and darkness. Twins, however, do not always bode ill. Among the Haida of the Pacific Northwest, for example, a creation myth tells a native version of the story of Beauty and the Beast: a beautiful young maiden falls in love with a bear and gives birth to twin bear cubs, who because of their extraordinary parentage are viewed as semi-divine beings. (Bill Reid, gold container, Canada, 1972: *far left*) Spider Woman, amongst the Hopi, gives birth to twin warrior sons who protect the people; other examples of helpful twins include Artemis and Apollo, and Castor and Pollux, the morning and evening stars. In France, *La République* (1848) is personified by Honoré Daumier as the Great Mother from whom the twin children of the free nation receive their nourishment and education.

The Face of the Waters

Of the four elements, water – ruled by the moon – is most frequently associated with the feminine. It is the waters of life that surround the unborn child, and the primordial waters that are the fountain of life. Waterways, wells, miraculous springs and mysterious lakes have always been a favourite haunt of the Goddess. At such places her slippery nature is revealed, as she is often reported to change form while bathing. There are a number of stories about the Goddess being spied on while bathing, and of the unlucky consequences of such actions. Nereids, naiads, nymphs and other water sprites, such as mermaids, all tend to be mischievous tricksters who delight in the nature of play, often at the expense of humans. (Venus with nymphs, Coventina's well, High Rochester, Northumberland, UK, 2nd–3rd c.; wooden carving of mermaid on misericord, Exeter cathedral, UK, c. 1230–70; limestone carving of dancing nereids, Delta region, Egypt, 6th c.)

In Mexico the Water Goddess is known as Chalchihuitlicue, the Goddess of the Jade Petticoat, who is said to have been responsible for the great flood that destroyed the world in the last age. (Pottery figure from Tajín,

4th–9th c.: *opposite, above left*) Like God, in the biblical story of the flood, Chalchihuitlicue, seeing that mankind had gone astray, made provisions for the chosen people to survive. She built a bridge from the fourth world to the fifth, on which they might pass to safety, and then sent a downpour of rain to destroy the evil doers. She was later remembered for her kind deed in sparing the righteous by great pilgrimages to her temple, where the people petitioned her for rain and water for the crops.

Amongst the Eskimo, the Ocean Goddess Sedna is both feared and loved. (Inuit stonecut print, 1961: *opposite, above right*) As Mother of the Seas, she provides an abundant source of food for the people; walrus, seals, fish and whales are all under her

guardianship. The prayers offered to her
ask for blessing in finding such
creatures and, more importantly, for
protection from the dangers that exist
in frozen waters. To offend Sedna by
deed or action could spell death for the
vulnerable Eskimo hunter.

In Japan, on the feast day of the
dead, thousands of little boats are filled
with food and messages for the
departed souls. Their spirits are then
invited to enter the boats, which are
gently set free upon the regenerating
water and sail through the gateway of
the Torii arch, Shinto symbol for the
Great Mother. The arch is both an
entrance and an exit, leading only back
to the Mother of Life, making it a
perfect sanctuary for wandering souls.

All Things that Grow

All things that arise from the Earth in the form of vegetative life mirror the great generative function of the Goddess. (Indian tree spirit, Bharhut stupa, 2nd c. BC) The process of transformation that is possible in mortal woman mirrors the miracle of growth that occurs in Nature. The fertile soil, the planting of the seed, the warmth of the sun and the falling of the rain give way to blossoming and maturity in the fruits of the harvest, before all returns to the Earth from which it came. At the beginning of this century, when the Douanier Rousseau envisioned *The Dream* (1910), he reinterpreted the age-old theme of woman as Nature by depicting an obviously civilized, but naked white woman surrounded by an abundance of lush vegetation and animals. She is being enchanted by the flute-playing of her dark native sister, lest she forget where her true origins lie.

The Tree of Life and the Goddess are one and the same. The Sumerian White Goddess Belili, or Beltis, was the patroness of all trees, especially the willow, emblem of Artemis and Kuan Yin, and here we see her as twin winged figures, bestowing blessing on the Tree of Life. (Relief from Nimrud, Assyria, 884 BC: *right*) Belili would later be masculinized by the Semites into Baal, who became the devil and the source of the Beltane festivities.

The Hopi Indians show the Corn Goddesses, who tend to the young plants in order to ensure their growth. (Spotted corn germination, acrylic painting, 1975: *opposite, below left*) On the far left is the Blue Corn Spirit, and next to her, the Spotted Corn Spirit. The two figures in the centre are pregnant corn spirits who bring fertility and germination; on their bodies are the spiral migration symbols, and they are standing upon the steps that

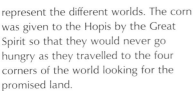

represent the different worlds. The corn was given to the Hopis by the Great Spirit so that they would never go hungry as they travelled to the four corners of the world looking for the promised land.

As the patroness of wheat, Ceres, known as Demeter in Greece, is the Earth Mother who provides a fruitful store with which to feed all her creatures. With the cornucopia in her right hand, and in her left a plaited wand of wheat, she came to symbolize the abundant generosity of the Roman state. (Ivory allegorical relief, 5th c.: *above right*) Agricultural peoples still make effigies to invoke the blessings of the deity. The Corn Goddess of the American Indians, the corn-dollies of wheat-growing peoples and the Rice Goddess Dewi Sri of Bali are fine examples of how the plant itself is turned into the body of the Goddess. These dolls or idols, made in the image of Ceres, are part of the seasonal festivities and are thought to bring the people a bountiful crop and good fortune throughout the year.

Lady of the Beasts

As the Great Mother, the Goddess nurtures and befriends all things; it is part of her natural instinct, which is both animal and divine. Through her relationship with wild and often dangerous animals, she serves as a bridge linking humankind with the world of Nature, for she transforms the fear we have of our animal drives and unites these untamed instincts with the expectations of our spiritual nature.

The image of a human figure flanked by two beasts is an ancient piece of heraldry that goes back to the Great Mother of Çatal Hüyük. From there it has spread to many cultures around the world, sometimes with a woman at the centre, sometimes a man. (Archaic Greek terracotta, Boeotia; embroidered linen towel end, Northern provinces, Russia, 18th–19th c.) In the Middle East this Three-in-One could represent the Mountain Goddess with her lions and, later, with her goats (ivory unguent box from Minet el-Beida, Canaan, 14th–13th c. BC: *opposite, above left*), or Lilith with her owls ('Burney plaque', Sumer, 2000 BC); elsewhere, her horses tell us that we are dealing with the Celtic Epona (stone carving, Beihingen, Germany),

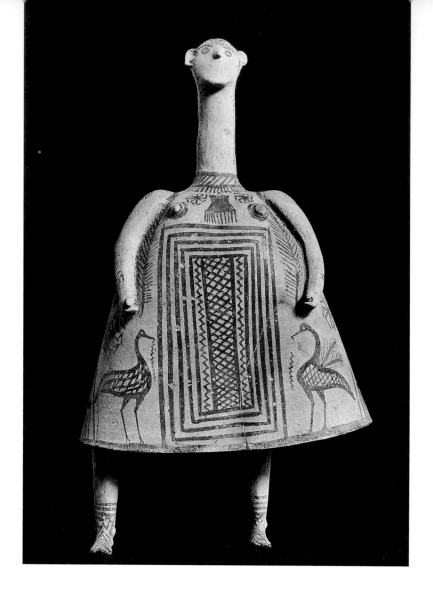

while in South America she is back with her dangerous feline allies. (Bronze ornament, Diaguite region, Argentina, 1100–1400) Whatever her name, it is clear that she rules over the double nature of the pair as it comes together in sexual union.

Anthropologists record the cross-cultural phenomenon of a link between the Mistress of Animals and the hunting rites of men: offerings are made to the spirit of the animal, totemic relationships are called upon, purification rites are performed, and dreams invoked to join hunter and hunted. (Rock drawing from Tiout)

Human Animal Divine

The divine feminine has always been linked with animals; from the insect world, as a bee, wasp or spider, to the domesticated cat, dog, horse and pig, on to the wild beasts of jungle and forest, and into the mythical realm of dragons and unicorns, the sphinx,

sirens and mermaids. The human inclination to adopt animals as spirit guides is evident in the totemic systems of people around the planet; these affiliations of kinship are believed to infuse the psyche with a variety of qualities, such as cunning, courage, vision and strength.

The spirit of a particular animal is often taken to represent a divinity, especially in Egypt, where this symbolic mode was all-important. There we find Mut, the vulture-headed Goddess, who was later transformed into a cat, now called Mut-Bastet. (Relief from tomb of Ankh-s-ka-re, c.2000 BC) As the vulture Goddess, like the winged priestesses of Çatal Hüyük (reconstruction drawing of funerary rite), she presided over the rites of the dead, and as Bast the cat – with her sistrum or rattle in her hand – she inspired the most celebrated festival in Egypt (bronze statuette holding sistrum and aegis: *right*). Thousands of people were said to line the banks of the Nile as her representative went by, all shaking their rattles, drinking, dancing and playing music. The sound of the orgiastic festivities was reported to be almost deafening. Serket, the scorpion

80

Goddess, was also connected with a
funerary cult, but as the one associated
with the healing powers required to
cure venomous bites, she was equally
patroness of medics. (Head of bronze
staff, Late Dynastic, XXVI–XXX;
Samarran pottery design of women and
scorpions, Iraq, 5th millennium BC) In
Greece this relationship between
poison and remedy would be
symbolized by the caduceus, where
twin snakes entwined on the Tree of
Life became the symbol for physical
and spiritual health.

In the New World, the eternal give
and take of the Goddess is represented
by the Serpent Skirt Goddess of the
Aztecs, Coatlicue, who stands for the
ancient wisdom that there is no life
without death, and no immortality
without self-sacrifice. (Stone sculpture,
Late Post-Classic, Mexico)

Hearer of Cries

Imbued with supernatural power
And wise in using skilful means,
In every corner of the world
She manifests her countless forms.

(Lotus sutra)

Throughout the world it has always been an aspect of the divine feminine who is invoked in times of need. The Goddess in her merciful manifestation is all-forgiving and compassionate towards the cries of her children. In China she is Kuan Yin, 'She Who Hearkens to the Cries of the World', who has been worshipped for well over a thousand years. (Blanc de Chine, late 18th c.) In Tibet her feminine form is Tara the wisdom-teacher. As the Bodhisattva of Compassion, she is infinite in her capacity to attend to the

needs of the people. Seated in the posture of 'royal ease', she holds a lotus sceptre in her hand which contains the Nectar of Wisdom, known as *amirta*; this she sprinkles on the heads of all who invoke her aid.

Amongst the Mayan peoples, Ixchel is the Goddess of Rainbows, Truth, Beauty, Healing and Childbirth. (Pottery figure from Campeche, Mexico, Late Classic period: *below left*) Like Kuan Yin, she sits in a royal pose, a crown upon her head, with her arms held open to embrace all who come to her. On the Yucatan peninsula, at the site of Tulum, dozens of murals have been found, showing various stages of childbirth. Tulum is thought to have been an initiatory pilgrimage place for women, where the mysteries of healing and birth were taught. The temples look out across the ocean waters to the Island of Cozumel and, to the north, towards the Isla Mujeres, or Isle of Women. Both islands have temples dedicated to Ixchel, who was the central figure in the rites of the Mayan women.

Another Goddess of Truth, Justice and Right Action is Maat of Egypt. (Wood relief from tomb of Sethos I, XIX Dynasty: *opposite, above left*) She is also called the 'Breath of Divine Life', and it is recorded in the Papyrus of Ani that 'the Goddess Maat embraceth thee both at morn and eve', meaning that she is present at both birth and death. It was she who, in the Hall of Two Truths, weighed the souls of the dead by placing them on the scales of justice, balancing them against the ostrich feather in her hair. She personified all that was right, just and in keeping with the basic laws of natural order and cosmic harmony.

In the West the image of the merciful Goddess is kept alive through Mary, the Mother of God, who intercedes on behalf of all sinners. (G.B. Tiepolo, *The Immaculate Conception*, 1767–69: *above right*) Over the centuries she has appeared to numerous ordinary people, particularly women and children, and has been the source of healing miracles throughout the world. Wherever she has manifested there are reports of numinous light, springs of water and heavenly scents. Here we see her surrounded by cherubim, standing on a

crescent moon and a dragon-snake,
which is pierced by the lily, emblem of
her purity. Above her head, the dove of
inspiration hovers to bestow the gift of
conception, reminding us that even
God required the body of a woman in
order to become human. The Western
world also created St Sophia as the
personification of Divine Wisdom.
(Drawing based on a 16th-century
Russian icon of the School of
Novgorod, by Jacqueline Klemes: *below
left*)

The healing power of women's
wisdom is also revealed by a clay urn
found at Monte Alban in Mexico
(Classic period), which shows a female
figure with a jaguar mask on her head.
Her devotional posture suggests that
she is a priestess in the Jaguar Cult,
which is intimately connected with the
mysteries of women. The jaguar
priestesses are solar shamans who
transform themselves into jaguars while
they perform their healing services.
Present-day Indians of the area still
acknowledge the power of the jaguar
by hanging jaguar-teeth necklaces
around the necks of their children to
protect them from harm.

The Goddess as healer, and as
compassionate mother who forgives all
trespasses, is evident in each of these
serene figures.

Bringer of Death

When Charles Darwin invoked the principle of natural selection to account for the origin of species, he was making use of the traditional insight that life feeds on death. Yet he failed to acknowledge the equally old tradition that saw woman as the representative of Nature and recognized Nature as the Goddess. We see this acceptance of Nature's darker side in Neolithic tombs, where the image of the Goddess is carved into the walls of the funeral chambers (Vallée du Petit Morin, Marne, France), and in Egypt, where the lid of the sarcophagus shows the bare-breasted sky Goddess Nut offering comfort to the dead. (Tomb of Ankh-nes-nefer-ib-re, Thebes,

XXVI Dynasty, c.525 BC) Elsewhere we find her in a variety of forms, from the grotesque to the humorous, always reminding us that death is the inevitable result of life. (Icon of Chāmundā, Orissa, India, 11th c.: *opposite, above*)

In Mexico she is Coatlicue, Lady of the Serpent Skirt and Mother of all Deities, the one who brought life and the one who would take it away. (Aztec statue of basalt, 15th c.: *opposite, below left*) Even the Saviour of the Americas, Quetzalcoatl, cannot deny the call of the Devouring Mother and laments: 'Our Mother the Goddess with the mantle of snakes, is taking me with her as her child. I weep.' Death has now become the enemy of man, who seeks immortality through conquering the forces of Nature. In

male mythologies the time-honoured function of the Goddess is no longer respected, but feared, and the Goddess as crone is viewed not as a wise woman but as an evil witch, who maliciously devours her children.

The Gorgon Medusa, initially part of a triad of Goddesses, has traditionally been represented as a terrifying monster, with her serpent locks and petrifying gaze. (Terracotta altar relief, Syracuse, late 7th c. BC) Yet her true message was one of wisdom, and had to do with the inevitability of death. The rising patriarchy, unwilling to acknowledge man's mortality, sent the hero Perseus to capture the steady gaze that mocked its pretensions to divinity. The benevolent nature that lies behind the 'evil' grimace of Medusa is revealed in her maternal embrace of the winged horse Pegasus, born from her blood when Perseus struck off her head.

Two, Three and Four

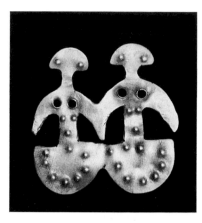

Certain numbers have long been sacred to the Goddess. At one time the mystic numeral seems to have been two, as we can see from twin Middle Eastern figurines (gold leaf ornaments, Alaca Hüyük, Turkey); this is surely an early form of Demeter and her daughter Persephone. Once there were likewise two Graces rather than three. (Raphael, *The Three Graces*, c.1500)

The Triple Goddess, in her aspects of Maiden, Mother and Crone, seems to be even more ancient. The Egyptians honoured her in the shape of Neith, 'that which is', Isis the 'Throne' and Selket, 'she who causes the throat to breathe' (gold figurines from tomb of Tut-ankh-aman, Thebes, XVIII Dynasty, c.1354 BC), while the Celts revered her

three-fold form as 'the Mothers'. She is not usually so distinguished in Christianity, though in the 16th-century German carving (School of Augsburg, Lower Saxony, Germany: *opposite, above right*), the addition of St Emerentia, apocryphal grandmother to the Virgin, along with her mother St Anne, carries on the old tradition.

In North America, however, the sacred number is four, and the Goddess accordingly appears in Navaho sand paintings as the embodiment of the four sacred mountains, or the four directions of space surrounded by the rainbow: *opposite, below.*

The Goddess is both the one and the many, yet even in her multitude of

forms she is but one Great Goddess. No
single aspect rules over any other, for
in all her diversity the Goddess
represents the full scope and power of
the feminine. The splintering of the
Goddess into many seemingly different
facets has led to a dilution of her
power, so it is essential that women,
who are the representatives of the
Goddess on Earth, take this multiplicity
into their lives and reveal it as a sign of
health and wholeness, rather than as a
fragmentation of feminine power.

The Light that Shines
in Darkness

The changing moon is the woman's star, whether it be thought of as feminine, as in the Old World, or as a man, as can happen in the New. In Cycladic figurines (1400–1200 BC) she appears in her two main forms: as the full moon, and as the crescent, whose horns remind us that from Paleolithic times the Goddess has constantly been associated with the bull and, to a lesser degree, other animals of the hunt. Venery, the old name for the hunt itself, tells of the ancient equation between sexual intercourse and the killing of animals. Hence the fate of Actæon the hunter, who mistook the time when women cleanse themselves each moon for that when the rites of Venus can be properly celebrated. (Attic krater by the Pan Painter, c.470 BC) He is killed by Artemis the Virgin Huntress, who is also the patroness of childbirth, and her emblem the moon fittingly honours the Virgin Mary and her child. (Albrecht Dürer, from the *Epitome in divae parthenices Mariae historiam*, 1511) In China, a similar intuition places the libidinous hare in the moon, where it prepares the elixir of life with a pestle and mortar. (Painting by T'ang Yin, Ming Dynasty)

Very different is the Aztec legend, which sees the quartering of the Moon Goddess Coyolxauhqui as a literal dismemberment at the hands of her heroic brother, Huitzilopochtli the war-god. (Stone relief, Tenochtitlan, early 16th c.: *opposite, above right*) This is part of the ascension to power of the masculine over the feminine, in which the feminine is transformed into

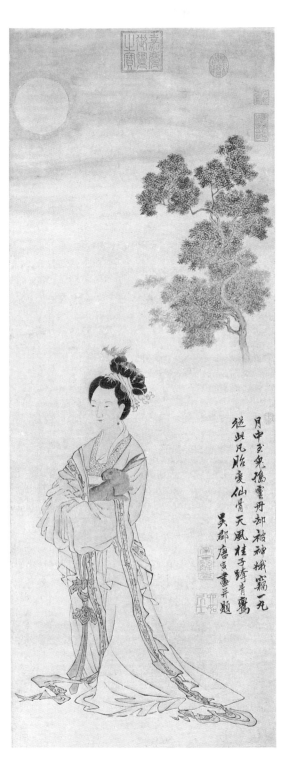

something evil – in this case, a wicked sorceress.

The full moon rising above the landscape is one of Nature's most enchanting images. (Samuel Palmer, *Harvest Moon, c.*1830) Seasonal festivities such as 'harvest home' are always celebrated at the time of full moon, and the cycle of eternal return is reflected in the bright face of the moon as she looks down upon the fruits of the land. The sickle-shaped tools used in harvesting the crops pay homage to the moon as the source of growth, for the very word 'crescent', from *crescere*, means to grow, produce or create.

Ever-watchful Eyes

Like any good mother, the Goddess keeps a watchful eye on her children. Eyes have always fascinated, charmed and bewitched, and sometimes the 'evil eye' has been cast towards those who offend, for the power contained in a glance can turn a man to stone. Old women in particular were thought to have perfected this ability, and during the Inquisition women accused of witchcraft were forced to enter the courtroom backwards to protect their judges from 'a look that could kill'.

Around 3000 BC the Goddess Ishtar had a temple built for her at Tell Brak in Syria; it was furnished with a multitude of small figurines, whose heads were reduced to enormous

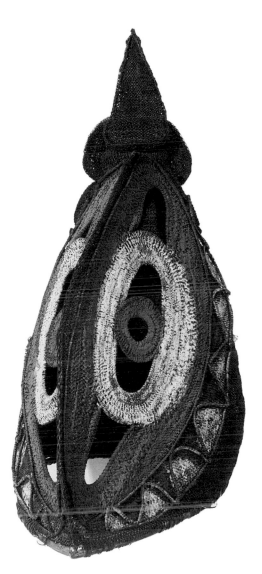

staring eyes. (Eye idol, c.3000 BC: *far left*)
We must suppose that at this moment
the Goddess became not only the
guarantor of the life of Nature, but the
overseer of a new form of social
organization, whose adherents are now
known as the megalith-builders. Their
traces can be found along the shores of
North Africa, in Ethiopia and up the
Atlantic seaboard as far as Ireland –
and everywhere the presence of the
Goddess is indicated by her all-seeing
eyes. (*Opposite*: vessel from Los
Millares, Spain, c.3000 BC; Anatolian
figurine, Turkey, c 2000 BC; double-
headed eye Goddess, Cappadocia, end
of 3rd millennium BC; *left*: eye-mask
used in menstruation rites,

Kwotmagum, Papua New Guinea,
1955–56)

The Egyptians knew her as the
Oldest of the Old, as the uraeus cobra,
or snake-tailed eye, from which all
things originated. (Pectoral ornament,
XII Dynasty, c.1991-1786 BC) This was
the emblem of sovereignty, which as
the sign of unlimited power could be
used as a talisman against the evil eye.
We also find the Goddess's eye as
prophylactic symbol in the form of the
Gorgon's head on Athena's shield, and
on the Greek drinking cup, where it
warns against the siren voice of
intoxication. (Attic kylix, Amasis Painter,
c.560–525 BC)

The Union of Opposites

With all the talk of a battle between the sexes, one would think that men and women were two different species, when in truth they are equally responsible for the fate of the world. Every culture provides us with insights into the balancing of feminine and masculine energies — Yin and Yang, Shiva and Śakti, the Earth Mother and Sky Father — while at the root of the most sophisticated philosophies lies the mystery of the sacred marriage rite. Of course, the *hieros gamos* must first take

place within oneself; then and only then is it possible to extend the concept of union towards another.

Images of God and Goddess, wife and husband, lingam and yoni speak to us of a dance between the Sun and the Moon, the Earth and the Sky, for all evolution depends on this coming together. There is a particular kind of beauty to behold when the male and female forces are in harmony. (Rameses III embraced by Isis, Thebes, c.1150 BC; Etruscan terracotta effigies on sarcophagus lid, Cerveteri, 6th c. BC; wooden carving of Dogon couple, 19th c.; Peruvian pottery couple, 1400–1532)

In Japan, agricultural peoples keep the praises of Dosojin (the man-woman deity) alive through numerous shrines that show the male and female together, sometimes as human figures, at other times as lingam and yoni. (Stones in Shizuoka Prefecture, Japan) Likewise, there is a sense of horror when this combined energy is used for evil. The two demons of death from India remind us that both women and men can perform acts of extreme ignorance and evil, capable of counteracting all the positive powers of the life force. (Vatapi and Ilvala, Mahakuteswar temple, 6th c.)

Spiders Spinning Spirals

Women and the Goddess have always woven, whether it be the weaving of cloth and the spinning of tales and spells, the weaving of tissue to bone inside the uterus, or the spinning of time and destiny in the universe. (Greek red figure vase painting, 6th–5th c. BC) Spinning wheels, spindle whorls, spiders and maze patterns are all part of the same motif. (Spindle whorl of carved maple, Coast Salish, North America, 19th c.; shelldisk with spider, Mississippian southern cult, Illinois, USA, c.1000 AD; coin with labyrinth symbol, Knossos, Crete, 1st millennium BC; *opposite, left*: maze of Chartres cathedral, 13th c.) Spiral dances lead us in and out of the labyrinth of life, as past, present and future are linked together by the thread of time, woven by the Fates, or Moirai: Clotho the Spinner, Lachesis the Measurer, and Atropos the Cutter of the Thread. They were believed to be present at the birth of a child to bestow the curses and blessings that would weave themselves into its personal destiny. In Scandinavia they were the Norns, or Weird Sisters, and the Valkyries, who used the blood and guts of men to weave the fate of the world.

Amongst the Navajo, the weaving of the world is in the hands of Changing Woman, or Spider Woman. She is responsible for maintaining the universe and for keeping the sacred dream of life alive. Even in the darkest hour when the web of life appears to be broken, she keeps on spinning and weaving. Spiders are therefore sacred to her and are never killed, for to do so is thought to insult the Grandmothers, or ancestors. Robed in black, they are associated with a special form of female magic that can be traced backwards in time, as well as projected into the future – but only through the

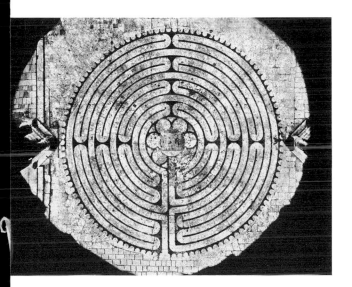

female line. (Colleen Kelley, *Return of the Grandmothers*, pencil on rag paper, 1984: *above right*) The Hopi also have their Spider Woman, whose two warrior sons are stationed at the north and south poles; together they protect the Hopi people and the Earth. (Acrylic painting, 1975)

Sources
and further reading

Agrawala, P.K., *Goddesses in Ancient India*, New Delhi: Abhinav Publications, 1984

Ardrey, R., *The Territorial Imperative*, New York: Atheneum, 1966

Bachofen J.J., *Myth, Religion and Mother Right* (1861), trans. R. Manheim, Princeton, N.J.: Princeton University Press/Bollingen series, 1967

Beauvoir, S. de, *The Second Sex*, New York: Bantam, 1961

Begg, E., *The Cult of the Black Virgin*, London: Arkana, 1985

Benedict, R., *Patterns of Culture*, Boston: Houghton Mifflin/Sentry, 1959

Binford, S.R. and L.R., *New Perspectives in Archaeology*, Chicago: Aldine, 1968

Blofeld, J., *Compassion Yoga: The Mystical Cult of Kuan Yin*, London: George Allen & Unwin, 1977

Briffault, R., *The Mothers*, 3 vols., New York: Macmillan, 1927

Burkert, W., *Greek Religion*, Oxford: Basil Blackwell, 1985

Crawford, O.G.S., *The Eye Goddess*, London: Phoenix House, 1957

Durdin-Robertson, L., *The Goddesses of Chaldaea, Syria and Egypt*, Enniscorthy: Cesara Publications, 1975

Eliade, M., *Gods, Goddesses, and Myths of Creation*, New York: Harper & Row, 1967

Fisher, E., *Woman's Creation: Sexual Evolution and the Shaping of Society*, New York: Anchor Press/Doubleday, 1979

Frazer, Sir J.G., *The Golden Bough: A Study in Magic and Religion* (1890), abr. ed. New York: Macmillan Paperbacks, 1960

Gimbutas, M., *The Goddesses and Gods of Old Europe: Myths, Legends and Cult Images*, London: Thames and Hudson, 1974

Goodale, J.C., *Tiwi Wives: A Study of the Women of Melville Island, North Australia*, Seattle: University of Washington Press, 1971

Graves, R., *The Greek Myths*, 2 vols., Harmondsworth: Penguin, 1955

—, *The White Goddess: A Historical Grammar of Poetic Myth*, London: Faber & Faber, 1948

—, *Adam's Rib and other Anomalous Elements in the Hebrew Creation Myth*, Clairvaux: Trianon Press, 1955; New York: Thomas Yoseloff, 1958

Harrison, J.E., *Prolegomena to the Study of Greek Religion* (1903), New York: Meridian, 1957

Hart, G., *A Dictionary of Egyptian Gods and Goddesses*, London: Routledge & Kegan Paul, 1986

Hawkes, J., *The Dawn of the Gods*, New York: Random House, 1968

Huxley, F., *The Way of the Sacred*, London: Star Books, 1980

Jacobsen, T., *Toward the Image of Tammuz and Other Essays on Mesopotamian History and Culture*, Cambridge, Mass.: Harvard University Press, 1976

—, *The Treasures of Darkness: A History of Mesopotamian Religion*, New Haven: Yale University Press, 1976

Kaberry, P.M., *Aboriginal Woman: Sacred and Profane*, London: Routledge, 1939

Kerenyi, K., *Athene: Virgin and Mother*, Zurich: Spring Publications, 1978

—, *Goddesses of Sun and Moon*, Dallas: Spring Publications, University of Dallas, 1979

Keuls, E.C., *The Reign of the Phallus: Sexual Politics in Ancient Athens*, New York: Harper & Row, 1985

Kropotkin, P., *Mutual Aid*, New York: Knopf, 1918

Lee, R.B., and I. DeVore (eds.), *Kalahari Hunter-Gatherers: Studies of the Ikung San and Their Neighbors*, Cambridge, Mass.: Harvard University Press, 1976

—, *Man, the Hunter*, Chicago: Aldine, 1968

Lerner, G., *The Creation of Patriarchy*, Oxford: Oxford University Press, 1986

Levy, G.R., *The Gate of Horn*, London: Faber & Faber, 1948

Lurker, M., *The Gods and Symbols of Ancient Egypt*, London: Thames and Hudson, 1982

Marshack, A., *The Roots of Civilization*, New York: McGraw-Hill, 1971; London: Weidenfeld and Nicholson, 1972

Mellaart, J., *Çatal Hüyük*, London: Thames and Hudson, 1967

—, *Earliest Civilizations of the Near East*, London: Thames and Hudson, 1965

—, *Excavations at Hacilar*, 2 vols., Edinburgh: Edinburgh University Press, 1970

Montagu, M.F.A. (ed.), *Man and Aggression*, New York: Oxford Paperbacks, 1971

Moon, S., *Changing Woman and Her Sisters*, San Francisco: Guild for Psychological Studies, 1984

Morris, D., *The Naked Ape*, New York: McGraw-Hill, 1967

Needham, J., *The Pattern of Nature-Mysticism and Empiricism in the Philosophy of Science: Third-Century BC China, Tenth-Century AD Arabia and Seventeenth-century AD Europe* (pamphlet), Oxford: Oxford University Press, 1953

Neumann, E., *The Great Mother: An Analysis of the Archetype* (1955), trans. R. Manheim, London and Boston: Routledge & Kegan Paul, 1963

Perera, S., *Descent to the Goddess*, Toronto: Inner City Books, 1981

Pjerrou, M., 'Hypatia, the Lost Philosopher' (unpubl. essay), 1987

Powdermaker, H., *Life in Lesu: The Study of a Melanesian Society in New Ireland*, New York: Norton, 1971

Preston, J.J., *Mother Worship: Theme and Variations*, Chapel Hill: University of North Carolina Press, 1982

Renfrew, C., *Before Civilization*, London: Jonathan Cape, 1973

Ruether, R., *Religion and Sexism: Images of Women in the Jewish and Christian Traditions*, New York: Simon & Schuster, 1974

Shuttle, P., and P. Redgrove, *The Wise Wound: Menstruation and Everywoman*, London: Victor Gollancz, 1978

Sjöö, M., and B. Mor, *The Great Cosmic Mother: Rediscovering the Religion of the Earth*, San Francisco: Harper & Row, 1987

Starhawk, *Truth or Dare: Encounters with Power, Authority and Mystery*, San Francisco: Harper & Row, 1987

Stone, M., *When God Was a Woman*, New York: Harcourt Brace Jovanovich, 1976

—, *Ancient Mirrors of Womanhood: A Treasury of Goddess and Heroine Lore from Around the World*, Boston: Beacon Press, 1984

Thompson, W.I., *The Time Falling Bodies Take to Light: Mythology, Sexuality and the Origins of Culture*, New York: St Martin's Press, 1981

Ucko, P.J., and A. Rosenfeld, *Paleolithic Cave Art*, New York: McGraw-Hill/World University Library, 1967

Vermaseren, M.J., *Cybele and Attis: The Myth and the Cult*, London: Thames and Hudson, 1977

Walker, B.G., *The Woman's Encyclopedia of Myths and Secrets*, San Francisco: Harper & Row, 1983

Weigle, M., *Spiders and Spinsters: Women and Mythology*, Albuquerque: University of New Mexico, 1982

Wheeler, Sir M., *Civilizations of the Indus Valley and Beyond*, London: Thames and Hudson, 1966

Wolkstein, D., and S.N. Kramer, *Inanna, Queen of Heaven and Earth: Her Stories and Hymns from Sumer*, New York: Harper & Row, 1983

Wollstonecraft, M., *The Rights of Woman* (1792) and John Stuart Mill, *The Subjection of Women* (1869), Everyman's Library, no. 825, New York: Dutton, 1955